Your Research Project

With ever increasing numbers of people going through higher education, and more and more working towards Masters degrees, the pressure on students to excel can be immense. Even for undergraduates, there is an increasing emphasis on project and research work, and success in your final project can make all the difference to the level of degree you achieve. Unfortunately, many students do not know how to manage on a day-to-day basis in this vital aspect of their course.

This book will help all students through the transition from passive learner to active researcher. It covers everything you need to know from

- selecting and refining a research topic,
- time and project management, to
- writing the actual report and preparing for a viva.

This book is the ideal guide for all final year undergraduates and students pursuing a Masters degree.

With straightforward, illuminating prose and a thorough understanding of the challenges and distractions that can plague a research student, Andy Hunt has created a truly indispensable guide.

Dr Andy Hunt is a lecturer in Music and Media Technology in the Department of Electronics, University of York, UK.

Your Research Project

How to manage it

Andy Hunt

Routledge
Taylor & Francis Group

LONDON AND NEW YORK

First published 2005 by Routledge
2 Park Square, Milton Park, Abingdon, Oxon OX14 4RN

Simultaneously published in the USA and Canada
by Routledge
270 Madison Ave, New York, NY 10016

Routledge is an imprint of the Taylor & Francis Group

© 2005 Andy Hunt

Typeset in Sabon and Gill Sans
by Graphicraft Limited, Hong Kong
Printed and bound in Great Britain by TJ International Ltd,
Padstow, Cornwall

British Library Cataloguing in Publication Data
A catalogue record for this book is available
from the British Library

Library of Congress Cataloging in Publication Data
A catalog record for this book has been requested

ISBN 0-415-34407-7 (hbk)
ISBN 0-415-34408-5 (pbk)

Contents

Illustrations

Preface

In over fifteen years of supervising students for their final-year university projects I have noted a gap in the market for a book for students to help them deal with the single most important and challenging part of their course. This book is intended to fill this gap.

At the start of a final project, students (particularly in science courses) are used to a steady routine that is well organised for them (extensive timetabled lectures, labs and assignments). Most are not equipped for the sudden transition into being completely in charge of a large and significant block of time where they become over-night, in effect, project managers.

It is my experience that a large part of the academic supervision process is focused on helping students to cope with this transition from passive worker to active manager. The problem is compounded by the fact that there are few people to delegate work to, so the student has to play the dual role of project manager and key worker, with almost no training, on perhaps the highest-marked assignment of their degree.

This book is therefore aimed at students and supervisors to help them become effective project managers who can plan, organise and execute their work, whilst gaining essential transferable skills in the process. It is intended that all final year, Masters, and Doctoral students should read this book prior to doing their project, then refer to it throughout the project period.

Acknowledgements

Many thanks are due to numerous students at the University of York, UK. Many of them inspired this work, and several have read and commented on it as they have been doing their projects. In particular, I would like to thank Alyte Podvoiskis, Trevor Agus, and Hector Scoursis for their extensive feedback in the early stages.

I have had many an inspirational chat with colleagues at York and round the world about projects, and management, but those that have really helped me to flesh out the ideas in this book are Ross Kirk, David Howard, Thomas Hermann, Marcelo Wanderley, and Andrew Cleaton.

Finally, thanks go to my family for bearing with me throughout this project – especially when the added burden of writing a book on top of a busy schedule made time management absolutely essential. I hope Amy and Tom feel as if I have spent a good proportion of time with them, and I wish them all the very best with organising their own lives as they grow. To my wife Caroline, who has not only held the fort and kept me going (and has occasionally threatened to turn the computer off late at night), but has also been my primary proof reader and copy editor as the book has developed, thank you!

Overview of the book

Chapter 1 outlines the important change in role that all students undertake when embarking upon a major project; they become both the Worker *and* the Manager. This chapter describes each role, along with some other common (not so useful) roles that people often play. The concepts outlined here are essential for the understanding of subsequent chapters.

In Chapter 2 we consider in some depth the issue of personal time management. On a solo project you are put in charge of a large block of time, and you need to use it wisely. This chapter includes some tricks and well-tried advice for making the most of the time you have available, and for balancing your work commitments with the rest of your life.

Chapter 3 takes you through the vital task of setting and refining your project's aims and objectives. We look at the process from choosing a project, then making it really yours. This chapter introduces several ideas for generating and managing creative ideas, and then communicating them to others in a clearly written proposal. We then discuss how to form the project title, the definition of aims, objectives, and a hierarchy of tasks.

Chapter 4 shows the importance of setting your work in context. We consider the different types of information source that are available nowadays, along with their relative advantages and disadvantages for research. We then discuss some of the different ways of putting together a literature survey.

In Chapter 5, you will see how to work towards success from the outset, by establishing in advance what makes a successful outcome at each stage of the project, and by considering how to map out the use of time over the project period. By the end of this chapter you should be able to produce a firm project specification and detailed time-plan, and have a clear idea of what the final project will deliver.

Chapter 6 deals with your communications with other people during the project period. We focus on the role of the supervisor, and offer hints as to how to maximise the benefits of the supervision process. There are included some points of advice about how to relate to other people whose help you may need along the way. Finally, we encourage you to think about the expectations of 'readers' and 'audiences' in preparation for talks and report-writing.

Chapter 7 looks at some commonly encountered problems (such as 'getting stuck' and 'losing motivation'), and provides practical guidance and suggestions for how to solve them.

In Chapter 8, we discuss the final report, thesis or dissertation. This chapter explains how to establish your readership, and present information in a logically ordered way to maximise the portrayal of your ideas to the reader. There is plenty of advice about how and when to write, and some warnings of common mistakes made at this point in the project.

Chapter 9 prepares you for the viva voce (or oral) exam. We consider what the examiners are looking for, and try to give you some insight into what it is like to be an examiner. Not everyone has to go through this process, but it is good practice to be prepared to explain and defend your work through talking about it.

Finally, Chapter 10 considers how you might publish the results of a successful project, and gives hints about conferences, journals and books.

Chapter 1

You – the project manager

Introduction

You are probably reading this book because ahead of you there is a major piece of work for which you are personally responsible. This book aims to help you through the process of managing this effectively.

Although this book is primarily intended for students in the final year of college or university embarking upon their solo or Masters project, the principles covered are the same for any piece of project work for which you do not yet feel prepared.

In this opening chapter we will examine your change in role from being essentially a reactive student to becoming a proactive project manager. We look at how the very nature of the work changes with a solo project, and acknowledge that many students are ill-prepared for this change. We then focus on the most important transformation that you will have to make, that is playing the role of *two* people. Once you can successfully flip between 'project manager' and 'project worker' in a structured way you will see your project starting to take shape. This chapter will help you to face up to the changes that need to be made in order to carry out your major piece of project work to a high standard.

Your change in role

Much of the work you have done up to this point may be regarded as *reactive*. You were given an assignment, told what the task was, given some starting information, given a strict deadline and guided as to how much work was expected of you. You then reacted to that information and provided a piece of work that fitted those specific criteria. Often this type of assignment is intended to test how you have absorbed and processed knowledge, and the boundaries of this information are usually defined for you in the syllabus. Most exams, essays and written assignments done at schools, colleges and universities are of this type.

And then comes the major solo project. This often represents a large proportion of the marks on a course, yet most students find they are unprepared for it. It is the pivotal point of a degree where the emphasis changes from responding to strictly defined tasks, to being in charge of an entire research project. It is as though for many years you have been a member of a backing group, reliably following written musical instructions along with your fellow musicians, and then suddenly you find you are running the show. What is more – the show does not yet exist. You find that you are no longer dealing with a pre-defined syllabus, and you are now engaging, by definition, with unbounded and possibly unknown material. You suddenly find there are no agreed right or wrong answers, and you may have to reconcile apparently contradictory information from others working in the area. You are often given one big deadline (the end of the project), and it is up to you to manage the entire business from now until then. It is no wonder that it can feel daunting. The purpose of this book is to help you through the process of transforming yourself from a diligent student into a dynamic and successful project manager.

The dual role (of Worker and Manager)

Perhaps the most important skill you will develop as part of running a solo project is playing two distinct roles; that of Worker and Manager. Most of us play different roles in different situations (e.g. student in lecture, friend in a social situation, leader of a group, parent, etc.), but rarely do we need to alternate between two roles in one situation. However, this is exactly what you will need to do in order to run a successful project. This section will help you identify what these roles are, and why both are important to the outcome of a large piece of work.

The Worker

You are in 'Worker' mode when you are just getting on with things. If you have made it to your final year, you are probably quite used to being a Worker because this is what your education system has trained you for. Being in Worker mode is a good thing *as long as you know* that this is the *right* thing for you to be doing at this moment. Unfortunately, the only way you are going to know what is the right thing for you to be doing is to have a higher-level picture of all the things you need to do, and their relative importance and timings. This is where the Manager comes in.

The Manager

All of us have experienced our inner Manager. Have you ever just *had* to sit down and make a list of things you needed to do, because there was so much floating around in your head? This is your inner Manager wanting to get some control of your life. You will sometimes feel the need to stop what you are doing and take stock of your progress on a number of topics that are lurking within your brain. This gives you the opportunity to get a bigger picture and set what you are trying to achieve into a higher-level context.

Dual, but mutually exclusive roles

It is really important that you do not mix the roles, or constantly flip between them. For example, when you are working on something (say, writing a chapter of a report) you really want to be in Worker mode where you *know* that it is absolutely fine for you to think of nothing else for the next two hours. However, you will only be able to get to that state if you have done some management activity first; for example, a weekly review process where you have considered all the topics that are ongoing in your life, along with their relative importance and urgency, and thus made a detailed plan for the week (which turns out, say, to include two hours of writing Chapter 1 on Friday). When you carry out a task you need subconscious reassurance that it is the right thing for you to be doing. Without this reassurance you will worry, panic and lose concentration, because your inner Manager cannot really rest until it has been through the process of putting everything in order.

Equally importantly, you will find that you cannot do your managerial tasks while trying to be a Worker. How can you think at a high-level about all the things you need to do while you are staring at a computer screen containing the low-level detail of the work, whether it is computer code or part of an essay? You need some time away from where you would do the project work. Sometimes this means literally moving somewhere else to get away from it; leaving the lab, shutting down the computer, or taking a pencil and some paper to a coffee bar, or going for a walk outside but taking a notepad; *anything* to remove yourself from the context where the Worker is normally active.

The Manage–Work cycle

You will need to develop a way of working that you feel comfortable with, but here is one method that you may wish to start with. For any new task, however big or small, allocate a proportion of time to *manage* it before you start *working* on it, and some time to review it once it is complete.

Let us take an example most of you will have had some experience with. You will probably be used to the exam technique of setting aside time at the start of an exam to read through the questions and make a plan for which ones you are going to answer and what approach you are going to take. Likewise you may have been advised to take time before the end of the exam to read through and review your answers. Those who practise this discipline are carrying out the Manage–Work cycle, in that they are setting aside some time to take stock of the big picture *before* focusing on the task at hand. This then gives them the confidence that they are working on the right things. After completing the work they then return to a managerial level to review what has been done. Nearly everyone who does this says that it is the best way to deal with exams, and yet every time they do it they have to fight off the nagging panic that they are 'wasting time' and should just be 'getting on with it'.

In general, it is best to apply a proportion of management time to *any* incoming task, *no matter how big*. This works for an urgent request that needs processing in the next ten minutes, and equally for a major project with a final deadline which is nearly a year away. Both cases require some calm, considered thought at a managerial level. Those people who are regarded as 'keeping their cool in a crisis' typically do this by insisting on a degree of planning even in the most desperately pressing circumstances. The general aim is to *insist* on planning time – even if this seems to be taking away from the time to do the task – because you can then proceed with the confidence that you are doing the *right* task. Once your working time is complete, you can go back into the management role, and review the completed work within a higher-level context. To summarise, it is good to run a project as a Manager, but to 'dip down' to a more focused Worker level for an allocated duration to complete one task, then 'come back up' to review progress.

In the next chapter we will look at some everyday examples from the world of projects to illustrate how this might work in practice.

Other roles to avoid

The dual role of the Worker and Manager is what is needed to get you through your project. It is important to keep these in balance. Too much management and nothing actually gets done! Too little management and the *wrong* things get done. However, as well as the Manager and Worker roles, there are other, less productive, roles that people can play during the lifetime of a project. Perhaps we should take a few moments to look at these in case you recognise some of the characteristics in your own methods of working.

The procrastinator

Procrastination is the act of putting off until some time in the future what should be done now. This is not to be confused with 'active deferral' – where a proper decision is made that this is not the time to do a particular thing. The procrastinator is so daunted by each new task they receive that they attempt to run away from either managing the task or working on it. Consequently, they fill their time with unrelated stalling activities. This can take the form of actively focusing on something totally unrelated, such as a social activity, or passively avoiding starting to work, for example sitting hopefully at a desk for long periods waiting for inspiration. Please do not misunderstand – life should have plenty of opportunities for socialising and daydreaming, but not as a masking activity that ultimately prevents you from making progress on your major piece of work. This is the Ostrich effect – the hope that by sticking your head in the sand the problem will somehow just go away. Sadly, procrastinators tend to go through life oscillating between a state of denial ('I *haven't* got a project to do, *honest*, I'll go for a drink instead') and panic ('Oh no, my 3000 word essay really *is* due in tomorrow morning'). Unfortunately, a solo project seems like an easy thing to procrastinate about; it is scary, it is big, and there is lots of time for stalling activity. It is amazing how fast time will pass, and the pressures of starting a project late and completing it under panic conditions are strongly not recommended.

If you have a tendency for procrastination the remedy is quite simple – you must *just start*. Once you have begun you have crossed the main hurdle, and you may even find the creativity beginning to flow. How many times have you put something off for ages, only to complete it in a few minutes and think, 'that wasn't so bad; why did I avoid it for so long?' If in doubt, just start with something small on the project. In later chapters we will discuss how to divide the project into manageable sections.

The perfectionist

Some people experience the opposite problem to the procrastinator – they can start easily, but can never finish 'because it's not perfect yet'. Perfectionism is a serious impediment to successful time management, and we will consider this in more detail in the next chapter. If, as a Worker, you over-run your allocated time in a vain attempt to make something perfect, you are now using up time that was allocated to another task. By all means strive for excellent work, but learn to stop at the end of your time-slot, *or* hop up to management level and have a conversation with yourself that should go something like this:

Worker: I need more time to get this right.
Manager: But we agreed to finish at 11.00am
Worker: Yes, I know, but it's not good enough yet, and I need more time.
Manager: But we have these other three tasks which have to be done this morning.
And so on.

It is probably best that nobody witnesses you having this conversation with yourself! (It is usually just a mental process where you weigh up alternative viewpoints.) Actually this is about the only time that you need to acknowledge the needs of the Worker and the Manager *at the same time*. Effectively, you are negotiating between the high-level context of the Manager, and the recent practical experience of the Worker. You will either come to the conclusion that the Manager was right, and you need to move on to the other tasks, *or* you decide that improving the current piece of work really *is* more important than doing the tasks you originally planned. Either way this is a *management decision*. The Worker makes a request, but the Manager decides.

To overcome any of your perfectionist tendencies you must stop when your Manager said you should stop (because it is *never* going to be perfect), or hold a management-level meeting to decide if the current priorities are correct.

The dependent worker

This is a Worker who has not yet accepted that they also need to be a Manager. They refuse the managerial role, and therefore constantly look to others to provide the structure that they are lacking. Later in the book we will examine the role of the supervision process, but the dependent worker does not use it properly. Instead, they pester their supervisor and insist on being told what to do, exactly how much to write, which papers to look at, how to spend their time, what is the 'correct' method, etc. So, instead of growing in confidence with their own managerial skills they become dependent on other 'gurus' or 'experts'. However, as most supervisors will tell you, the idea of the supervision process in a solo project is to turn *you* into the expert for your particular topic, and to decrease your reliance on others.

If you find yourself feeling like this, it is probably because you are so used to being told what to do that you find it hard to acknowledge that you are now in charge. What you must trust is that playing the management role is ultimately very fulfilling. It is this role which makes it become *your* project, and in the future you will look back on the solo project as one of the most rewarding growth experiences of your entire education. People have often described it as 'learning to grow up'.

The over-keen worker

You might find it strange that a book about successful projects should criticise students for being over-keen. Many times students are so enthusiastic with the initial excitement of a project that they omit the managerial level in a misguided attempt to use all of their available time in 'getting on with it'. Many people when faced with a large and daunting project do a very silly thing – they just dive straight in and start working. From my experience of supervising software projects I know this is a particular problem. It seems to be a specific temptation when computers are involved – when faced with a large task, why not just sit down at the computer and start coding? But how do you know what you should be working on? Only when the project folds in on itself because it is too complex, do these people realise their mistake. Sometimes it is then too late. The over-keen Worker must insist on being driven by their Manager, so that they can then channel their enthusiasm into the *right* work.

Summary

This chapter has introduced a concept that will be referred to throughout the book – that in order to complete a project success-fully the whole process needs to be *managed* well. This management role is different from the equally important task of *working* to actually get the project done. You must play both roles, and be willing to change between them, yet keep them in balance. While you are reading this book you will probably be in 'management mode', as by definition you are not 'getting on with it'. However, many years of experience have shown that those students who take the time to train themselves to be effective self-managers are those who produce the best projects.

I wish you success from the start. In the next chapter we will look together at the basic problem the Manager has to face – dealing with time.

Chapter 2

Personal time management

Introduction

In this chapter we will consider in some depth the issue of how to manage your own time in the context of a major solo project. You have been put in charge of a large block of time, and you need to use it wisely. This chapter discusses some well-tried advice for making the most of the time that you have available, and for balancing your work commitments with the rest of your life.

The most important thing to acknowledge is that you cannot actually manage time! The phrase 'time management' is a bit of a misnomer, because time just moves on regardless of what you do. Better phrases would be 'time awareness' or 'self-management', as the only thing we can do with time is to acknowledge that it happens, and react accordingly. It is rather as if you were a canoeist, battling to stay afloat in turbulent water, and claiming that you were doing 'river management'. In reality the river is just *happening* and there is nothing you can do to manage or control it. However, you *can* deal with the tiny part of the river that you are in momentary contact with. You *can* control how you respond to the river, and you can use your paddle and the angle of your body to prevent yourself from being thrown onto the rocks or submerged, which is what would happen if you did nothing.

So, time moves on, and the only part of it we have any contact with is the present moment. Yes, we can *review* what is gone (the past), and *plan* for what is coming up (the future), but the actions we take now (the present) are the only things we can really control. So time management is really about managing the actions we take from moment to moment, weighing up what *has* happened and pointing ourselves in the direction of what we *want* to happen.

This is why the central question of all time management systems is 'what is the *right* thing to do *now*?' We will return to that question later in the chapter, but first let us consider again your changing managerial role as you take on a solo project.

Reactive time management

Typically, students are driven by their timetable; the schedule of lectures, tutorials, lessons, supervisions, practical sessions and exams which are produced for you by your place of learning. Your experience of this will differ according to which course or institution you are enrolled with.

Some courses are lightly loaded, with only a few scheduled sessions per week. These tend to give you some practice in time management skills as your main task may be, for example, to prepare for a seminar in three weeks time. If you are used to this type of course, you will probably be comfortable with the concept of setting your own schedule. Your biggest problem will be in coming to terms with just how *much* needs to be done for a solo project, and realising that you will need to generate all the actions and deadlines yourself.

Other courses, in dramatic contrast, schedule every hour of the working day with taught sessions, laboratories, back-up courses, and supervisions. In addition to this, they often have a high assessment factor, with many continuous assignments active at any one point, and several courses to revise for examination. Students on this type of course may *feel* as if they are practising intensive time management, because they are constantly aware of how much there is to do and how little unscheduled time they have to do it in. However, they are in for a shock when they come to the solo project, as this frantic structure disappears. There is no daily scheduling prepared for you; only an empty calendar and one big deadline at the end of the project. The good news is that you will be used to intensive work and handling many different tasks, so many of the techniques that follow may seem familiar. This will help you to create your own detailed schedule to fill the empty calendar.

Proactive time management

Now that you are the Manager for a solo project, you are solely responsible for deciding what you do every month, every week and every day. You will have many different tasks (or threads of activity) to do, but you need to define them all. You will have been given a final deadline (and possibly some interim deadlines) but there is a lot of time between now and then. Like our imaginary canoeist, if we do nothing we will drift with the flow and capsize or hit the rocks. Instead, we need to be *proactive* at every stage. Then, you can learn to use the power of the river's flow to take you where you want to go. The more you practise, the better you can steer yourself in the correct direction, and handle the turbulent flow. So it is with time management.

From the previous chapter you will be aware of how important it is to be able to plan thoroughly, so that you can switch *off* the Manager mode, and act as the Worker for set periods of time to actually make the project move along. So the three main skills of proactive time management are:

- to know what has happened so far
- to identify what needs to be done
- to organise the upcoming tasks so that the Worker handles them effectively.

These three skills could be referred to as *review*, *plan*, and *organise*. Look out for them throughout the rest of the chapter. In the next section we will examine the basic time management techniques, which will give you the methods for carrying out your reviewing, planning and organising.

Methods of time management

Many books have been written on this subject, and each has a particular flavour. Some assume you are a high-powered executive with secretaries and personal assistants at your service (e.g. Godefroy and Clark, 1991). These often focus on how to delegate tasks effectively to other people. As a student you do not have this luxury, but the job of a Manager is to delegate well-thought-out tasks to a Worker. It is just that both jobs now fall to *you*. Other books are written for people busy trying to manage conflicting life goals such as looking after children and carrying out a career (e.g. McGee-Cooper, 1994 or Morgenstern, 2001). You may fall into this category and so may find such books worth reading. In short, there is now a wide range of books (and audio programmes on tape or

CD) available, each with its own target audience and favoured methodology. Very little has been written for the student, and less still regarding this final phase of your course – the project. So how do you go about choosing a method?

The most important thing to realise is that almost *any* method is better than *no* method. Anything that gets you thinking about your priorities and tasks, and discusses how to handle deadlines, appointments and discretionary time will help you to improve your skills. However, the most common (and somewhat ironic) cry is, 'I don't have any time to study time management'! Whilst this may appear to be a perfectly logical response, it is rather like someone who has fallen in the sea telling the lifeboat crew to go away, saying, 'I am too busy trying to stay afloat to be rescued'. Time management techniques *are* the rescue team which can help you escape from either having too much to do, or not knowing how to handle your time.

Different time management methods suit different personalities and job roles. Your preferred method may well change as you change job, or as you develop as a person. The rest of this chapter takes a look at what these techniques all have in common, and then adds some specific advice that will be helpful for you in your dual role as a Manager–Worker.

Most time management methods encourage you to do the following five things:

- get your life goals established
- know what you are committed to
- define what needs to be done to make this happen
- prioritise these according to importance and urgency
- learn to control the 'new stuff' coming into your life.

Let us look at each of these in turn.

Get your life goals established

It is really important that you take time to think about what you want to achieve in life, and what your priorities are. We will assume that part of your life's ambition is to successfully complete your current course (if not – then stop reading now, and go and do some serious top-level thinking). A major part of achieving this goal is to carry out your solo project effectively. So this book will assume that you want to do well in your project, and that is what we will concentrate on. However, you may wish to look at some of the reading material referred to in the bibliography to help you look at your life goals in some more detail.

Know what you are committed to

Before you can prioritise or schedule your tasks, you first need to establish what jobs you have to do. If you have ever felt compelled to write down a list of what you needed to do (a 'To do' list), then you were probably trying to tame the sense of internal panic that hits everyone when they feel they have too much to do, or they realise that what they have to do has not been properly defined yet.

A 'To do' list is a reasonable way of helping you capture the fleeting information that bubbles up inside your head, but it is not very effective as a time management tool. The main problem is that your brain will 'throw' things at the list without any apparent order or relationship. A typical 'To do' list might look like this:

    Mend puncture
    Shopping
    History assignment
    Call Jack
    Tea, sugar, milk
    Start project
    Set video
    Torch batteries

You may instantly feel better having made such a list, because you have got things off your mind and onto paper. This is a good thing, and is one of the central tenets of David Allen's excellent book *Getting Things Done* (Allen, 2002). Allen also acknowledges that such lists on their own are useless for planning and organising. Let us consider five aspects of the above list to determine why this is:

1   How do you know that the list contains *all* the things you need to do? If you are not sure, then how could you trust it as a basis for planning what to do next? There will always be a nagging doubt that you might need to be doing something else more important.

2   The *order* of the list was simply the order your brain thought of the items. It is highly improbable that it is ordered in a sensible way. Is mending the puncture somehow more important than the history assignment, and even more so than starting the project?

3   Some of the items might *relate* to each other, if only they were to be re-organised. Maybe 'Tea, sugar and milk' and 'Torch batteries' are part of 'Shopping'.

4   The list gives you no clue on absolute or relative *timings*. What things need to be done by a particular time? What things ought to be done before other things? Maybe the puncture really does need mending before you can go shopping or hand in the assignment. But perhaps the video needs setting in the next hour if you are not to miss that special programme. Perhaps the History assignment should be completed before you start on the project, and this needs to happen before next Tuesday.

5   The *actions* are not well defined, and exist at many different levels. What exactly do you have to do to 'start project'? (Such vague list items are often the cause of procrastination; you do not start the project, because you have not yet thought out what that really means.) Presumably 'torch batteries' refers to buying some more, but unless this gets transferred to a shopping list, which you have with you when you are shopping, the batteries are likely to remain unbought.

Hopefully you can see that the 'To do' list (which many people, and some software organisers, regard as the only planning tool) is highly limited. To move beyond the 'brain-dump' level of a typical 'To do' list, you will need to address the five issues listed above.

To address the first point, you should take some time (in Manager mode) to establish the tasks that are in your life. The following questions might be useful to prompt you:

*   What things in life need doing by you?
*   What things have you embarked upon that you need to complete?
*   What tasks have you promised other people that you would do?
*   What would you like to do, but have not done anything about yet?

One of the best ways of getting a handle on all the different commitments in your life is the *project list*, and we will deal with this specifically later in this chapter, under 'Tools of time management'.

To address issues 2 to 5, your Manager will need to organise the raw responses to the above questions by re-ordering them, spotting relationships between them, considering their relative and absolute timing, and ultimately determining the actions that will need to be carried out by your Worker. Let us now look at some techniques to help you do this.

Define what needs to be done to make this happen

Given that you have identified those things in life that you are committed to, most time management systems give you some techniques for making sure that those things happen.

At the most basic level, it seems that the human brain is not very good at seeing 'the big picture' at the same time as it is looking at very specific details. Therefore we need tools and techniques to help us externalise our thought processes. Issues 2 to 5, above, give some indication of how the raw tasks need to be processed in order for us to know what to do. In other words you need to do most of your planning and thinking at Manager level, so that your Worker does not have to think about anything else other than the task in hand.

The specific tool we mention later under 'Tools of time management' is the *action list*. This is like a highly specialised 'To do' list, but one that has been managed effectively so that your Worker can trust it as being reliable and accurate.

Prioritise these according to importance and urgency

Once you have a list of actions that need doing, you should consider their relative priorities. Which one is most important to do at this time? This also requires knowledge of relative timing. Which ones are due by a certain date and can only be done in advance of that date? Which ones can only be done *after* another action is completed? Which ones are actually optional?

Once the relative priorities and timings are sorted, these can be marked on the action list, or entered into the *calendar* and *daily* *planner* (the other two tools for time management that will be discussed later in more detail).*

Learn to control the 'new stuff' coming into your life

The final issue that most time management methods urge you to deal with concerns the *inputs* to your life. The theory goes that once you acknowledge just how much you are already committed to it will be easier to deflect any new unwanted inputs. Inputs come in the guise of new *tasks* such as, 'Ah hello, I was wondering if you could help me . . .', as well as *information* that needs processing, in the form of email, post, phone calls, voicemail and interruptions (by others and by yourself).

You owe it to yourself to learn when it is appropriate to say 'no' to a new task. Once you have completed your project list, which shows all the active commitments in your life, you will be able to say in all honesty, 'I cannot take on that task with my current level of commitments'. If you really *have* to take on the new task (because it is essential to your goals, or somebody more senior insists) then you have every right to reconsider your project list, and see what project currently on the list can be cancelled, or delayed. You can even give this back to the senior person, saying, 'If I have to do this, could you help me by relaxing the deadline on another project, or cancelling one of these?' It may help to show them one of your project lists so that they can appreciate the extent of your current commitments.

You can deal with the new information which constantly streams into your life by becoming an expert at removing things as fast as possible. David Allen urges (and I can support this personally) keeping your email inbox empty! Every time you check your email, and there is a new batch of messages, move them out of your inbox immediately.

The messages will be one of the following:

• Junk mail – so take pleasure in deleting whole batches of them.
• Unwanted mail – you need take no action on, and you do not wish to keep, so DELETE it.

* Some people prefer to keep a simple diary. This acts as a calendar to remind you not only of appointments, but also tasks which need completing on a certain day or within a certain week.

- Information that you wish to keep, so FILE it by copying it into a folder (making a new folder if you need to).
- Mail which needs some action, but can be done quickly – so DO IT NOW, then DELETE it.
- Mail which needs action, but also needs significant further thought that would distract you if you did it now, so copy it to a special ACTION folder.

There are no other categories. As long as you regularly check your Action folder, and build these actions into your plans, this will give you a clear Inbox and a clear head.

Do similar things with mail and voicemail. If you have a physical inbox (such as a tray on your desk for collecting incoming mail and other papers), schedule regular time to keep it clear, and do not use it for storage.

If you do these things as a matter of course you will reduce the inputs into your life, whilst at the same time removing a lot of the clutter, and ultimately become responsible for what you *do* let in.

When to work, and for how long

You probably already have a good idea of when you do your best work. Some people are 'morning people' and they have a couple of hours of creative flow after breakfast. Others are 'night owls' who work most effectively late into the evening. Figure 2.1 illustrates a typical pattern of daily energy levels, but everyone is different. It is essential that you establish what your peak working times are

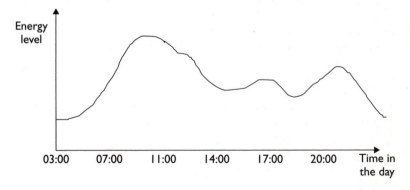

Figure 2.1 Typical daily energy levels

(as there may be more than one) during a typical day. Conversely, you should have an honest appraisal of when you are useless (often this is in the few hours after lunch, or in the early evening).

Now that you have some idea of your varying energy levels during the day, you can allocate activities accordingly.

- Your very best times should be given to your Manager, as this is when you need to be most mentally alert. When your management tasks are complete, allocate the remainder of your peak time to the Worker for special creative tasks. Many people waste this peak time by watching television, reading the paper, checking email, browsing the Internet, or chatting to friends. There is nothing wrong with these activities in themselves, but in order to maximise your productivity you should really do them when you are not fit for anything else.
- Give your good-to-moderate times to your Worker, as in this mode you only have one thing to focus on, but you do need *some* level of concentration.
- Give your least attentive, lowest energy, times to non-critical activities – preferably resting or having fun. If you have so much to do that you simply *must* work during these times, make sure that you allocate activities with a low mental load (see Figure 2.2).

You may be amazed at the difference that you can make to your effectiveness just by allocating the appropriate tasks to the right times. Most people gradually discover a 'magic time' when they can get through an immense amount of work. Guard that time against interruptions, and use it well to make progress on your most important tasks. As an added bonus, you may find that you complete your work faster, and that you gain lots of extra time. This feature is further enhanced by the rule we now consider.

The 80:20 rule

Most of the time management books quote the 80:20 rule. It appears in various guises, but its basic claim is revolutionary:

> '80% of a task is completed within 20% of the typical time allocated to it'

Energy level	Typical activities to allocate
Peak	Setting aims and objectives Managerial review Planning the day Creative work (e.g. creating a contents page for a report, or planning the outline structure of a piece of work) Checking work before submitting it
Moderate	Writing large chunks of text Reading reference material Checking and responding to email, post, etc. Meetings with supervisor, colleagues, etc. De-bugging computer code
Low	Fun activities Non-critical meetings with people (as having other people present will provide stimulation to counteract tiredness) Walking to collect things (e.g. books from library), as exercise helps invigorate a tired mind and body 'Paper-shifting' tasks which do not require much thought (such as working through a set of hand-written questionnaires and typing them into a computer)

Figure 2.2 Allocation of activities to times of differing energy levels

The implications of this are astounding. If it is true, it means that most of us could carry out the majority of our work in one-fifth of the time! It also implies that the remaining 80 per cent of the time is spent refining, adjusting and making only small improvements. It is certainly worth challenging yourself to work more effectively, and create more free time for you to spend as you wish.

Let us take an example; imagine you had the large task of writing up a five-chapter report. Most people would naturally allocate several weeks for this. But what if you only had one week? Well, it would have to be one chapter per day. But how much of each day do you wish to spend working on it? You may wish to allocate certain key times (e.g. one hour in the morning) for planning, and sketching out the structure. Then, let us say you have 3 hours working time left in the day. You divide up the number of sections in the chapter by the time you have available, and that is how long the Worker has to do the writing. The Worker can then scope the writing accordingly, perhaps writing a given section in 20 minutes. When you are under such time pressure, just ask yourself, 'What is essential to cover in this section?', then take 20 minutes to do it.

Now imagine you only had 2 days to write the whole report. Think it through. Could you do it? What changes would you have to make? Would you actually have to work *harder*? Everyone assumes the answer is 'yes', but you could trade off the level of detail of what you write, and be happy with shorter sections, with less time for fine-tuning and revision. It is worth challenging yourself to discover how much time you *really need* to complete a task. In Chapter 1, we read of the perfectionist trap – always needing more time, never finishing and ironically never getting any satisfaction or 'closure' on a piece of work. Giving yourself a strict deadline is an effective tool for counteracting the problem of perfectionism.

Getting started

For some people the worst part of any project or task is actually getting started. We saw in Chapter 1 another of the negative roles that people play – that of procrastinator – always putting off what should be done.

One of the best methods of 'unsticking' such a project and making a start, is to allocate a small amount of time in one of your peak energy periods. When you find yourself in that allocated time-slot, you just insist that you write something. Often writing *anything* is better than writing nothing. This is partly because as soon as you have committed something to paper, you have something in front of you to amend, change or criticise. This sets up a creative 'loop' where you find you are making progress.

If you really have no idea what to write you may want to try one of the following 'tricks':

- List what you already know about the project.
- List what you want to achieve (this often turns into the final structure of the piece of work).
- Imagine a radio interviewer has just shoved a microphone in front of you and has asked, 'So then, what's this piece of work about?' Write down your answer, and keep it short. This is often a good starting point.
- Ask yourself, 'Are there some unanswered questions that are preventing me from getting on with this?', then write down the

questions. Now apply yourself to each question in turn and come up with some answers, or suggestions on how you might find those answers.

Sometimes, you will reach the end of the time period and wish you had longer to work on it. That is the time for a management decision; can I carry on now while the flow is happening, or do I have other tasks that I really need to tackle?

Many time management systems do not acknowledge the dual role of Worker or Manager. They encourage you to be constantly weighing up your priorities so that you know what the most important or urgent thing is; but this can interfere with the Worker getting on with the actual work.

This section has explained the importance of being aware of the rhythmic cycles of your own energy levels, and allocating work appropriately to different times of the day. We have also looked at some hints for getting started and for working effectively within deadlines to create spare time.

Tools of time management

Now that we have looked at some of the common issues of time management, we will examine a set of four tools that will help you to manage your work and enable the Manager and Worker to communicate effectively. The tools are:

- a calendar
- a tasks/project list
- an action list
- a daily planner.

This book gives you some specific examples of how to use these tools. Throughout the explanations you are encouraged to customise the entire process to suit your own temperament and preferences.* Be aware that for effective time management you need to know:

---

* Some people actively rebel against a formal list, others find it saves their lives! It is vital to develop a system that you will *use*. A simple system regularly used is far more effective than a complex one used half-heartedly.

- what *events* are already planned in your life (here called the calendar);
- what things you are *committed to* (here called the project list);
- what has to *happen* to carry out those commitments (here called the action list);
- what needs to happen *today* (here called the daily planner).

As long as these functions take place, it does not really matter what you call them. However, over the years I have noticed that many students have a diary or a computer organiser, yet do not use them to carry out those functions effectively. So here is a system which works well, and will get you very organised, but as you read it keep thinking if there are better ways for you to achieve the same functionality.

We look at each of these tools in turn in the following sections.

Calendar

A calendar is any system that holds details of appointments you have in the future. This could be a paper-based diary (although many people use diaries as notebooks, and as ways to record the *past*), or a computer program. The Manager needs to have a clear view of what is coming up at different time levels:

- over the lifetime of the project (see Chapter 5)
- this month
- this week
- today.

Every time you have a new appointment it should be entered into your calendar. Regular meetings and supervisions should go in there, as should any social commitments. Be very careful if there are multiple calendars in your life.* These very easily become unsynchronised, and you may not know the true state of your appointments and commitments. Also put in your calendar things you wish to be *reminded* about, e.g. project deadlines that you

---

* Some people have a paper diary *and* an electronic organiser *and* a family diary on the wall in the kitchen. Consider whether you can get away with fewer places to record your commitments, or establish a regular time when you synchronise the appointments in each place.

have set, television programmes you wish to watch, things which really need to be done on or by a particular day.

The Worker should only be concerned with the commitments for 'today' or in the near future, and for this reason it is advisable to use a special reduced calendar known as the daily planner (see later section).

Tasks/project list

Whilst the calendar holds all your scheduled appointments and deadlines, it is not a complete record of what you have to do in your life. It is vitally important that you have a trusted list of *all* the tasks, projects, commitments and threads of activity that belong to you.

Earlier in this chapter we criticised the 'To do' list as being a rather raw 'brain-dump', which needed much further processing before it became useful for planning purposes. We asked you to consider the following questions:

- What things in life need doing by you?
- What things have you embarked upon that you need to complete?
- What tasks have you promised other people that you would do?
- What would you like to do, but have not done anything about yet?

If you have spent some time answering these questions, you may have a long list of projects that have not yet been completed. It might look something like Figure 2.3.

History assignment
Choir rehearsals
Major solo project
   Literature survey
   Initial report
   Prepare aims and objectives for supervision
Prepare for Auntie Eve's visit
Decorate the spare room
End of term report
Etc.

Figure 2.3 An enhanced 'To do' list

Notice how you naturally split 'major solo project' into three sub-projects. Each of the sub-projects probably should be an entity in its own right on your project list.

Many people have forty or more of these commitments. However, when you first start making a list you may only be able to think of seven or so, but gradually things will pop into your head, and you can update the list.

There are many more tasks that are so ingrained into your life that you do not even consider putting them on this list:

- eat regularly (includes cooking and washing up)
- wash and keep clean
- travel regularly to destination
- wash and dry clothes
- tidy the house
- weekly exercise.

Whilst these are part of your life, and they take up time and energy, they probably do not need to go on the project list as you do most of them automatically. The project list is for things that you *want reminding about regularly*.

Eventually this project list gives you a written handle on all the different parts of your life where you have commitments. You should update it regularly, delete completed projects from it, and add new ones to it. Figure 2.4 is an expansion of the expanded 'To do' list (Figure 2.3) into a five-column table, with many more details added which are discussed below.

Please note that there may be better ways for you to store this information (for example in a more graphical form such as mind-maps, which are introduced in the next chapter). Whatever form you choose, the important thing is you are *not* relying on your head to store this information.

1   In the first column you list the project title, e.g. History assignment (this is often taken directly from your expanded 'To do' list).
2   In the second column you put a short description of the *intended outcome*. In other words, when this outcome has eventually happened you will know that you have completed this project. Sometimes this may be the same as the title, but at other times they differ remarkably. For example, if you are

Project list

Project	Outcome	Deadline	Next actions	Deadline
History assignment	Report written, proofread and submitted	4th May	Write last chapter Check references in library Proofread report Final printout Take to departmental office	20th Apr 23rd Apr 30th Apr 2nd May 3rd May
Choir rehearsals	Concert successfully given	10th August	Choose music Get music from library Put in folders Create rehearsal schedule Phone choir members	19th Apr 23rd Apr 24th Apr 26th Apr 26th Apr
Solo project: Literature survey	Good mark for Literature survey	10th May	Complete Internet search Check journal section in library Write plan for contents page	22nd Apr 23rd Apr 25th Apr
Solo project: Initial report	Hand in initial report promptly	2nd May	Read report specification Sketch basic sections	25th Apr 27th Apr
Solo project: Prepare aims and objectives for supervision	Establish aims for project, and agree them with supervisor	30th April	Brainstorm aims Type up aims and objectives Read them to Jim for feedback Email to supervisor in advance of meeting	22nd Apr 24th Apr 25th Apr 27th Apr
Prepare for Auntie Eve's visit	Auntie has nice time staying here	15th July	Phone bus company (enquire about cheap tickets) Decorate room (see next project)	3rd May 12th July
Decorate the spare room	Room comfortable before Auntie Eve arrives	12th July	Select colour scheme Buy paint Invite friends for painting party	5th May 7th May 10th May

Figure 2.4 Example project list

learning to swim you may simply have the project title 'Swimming', but the intended outcome is, 'Confidently swim two lengths, and float for two minutes', and you want this to happen before June because that is when you are going on holiday, so the deadline says 'June'.

3   The third column contains a deadline for this activity. Most time management systems stress the importance of setting deadlines. Either put in the deadline that you have been given, or estimate by when this thing really needs to be completed.

4   The fourth column is for the *next actions* on the project (described in more detail below).

5   The final column contains the individual deadlines for each 'next action'.

The 'Next actions' column encourages you to turn each project into a set of actions that the Worker could carry out without any further planning. You really do not need to identify *all* the actions needed to complete the project, but rather just the *next* one or two. It is advisable to give each of these actions a deadline (working backwards from the final deadline and allowing time for slippage) so that they can be given to the Worker in good time.

In summary, what you are doing with the project list is acknowledging all the commitments in your life, and then breaking them down into the next one or two concrete actions that need to be taken to keep them moving.

Action list

The third basic time management tool is simply a list of the actions (generated above at the project-planning level) that need to be carried out. This is used as the list of instructions that advises the Worker which day-to-day activities need to be carried out.

Action lists are more useful if they are ordered to suit your life, and to reflect the various priorities and relationships between them. Therefore you might want to group actions together that can be done in a particular context. For example, you could put under one heading all the things that you can do at your desk and/or computer. Under another heading might come all the things you can do when you are in the library.

This is a familiar trick to anyone who has ever made a shopping list. What you are effectively doing when you make a shopping list is bringing together a series of outstanding actions (get sugar, get milk, etc.) into one list that is uniquely useful *at the shop*. You do not put 'complete history project' on your shopping list, because there is little use in seeing that when you are at the shop. So, establish the main areas of your life where you need lists of actions.

If we take the above example project list (Figure 2.4), and carry out this process, it might start to look something like Figure 2.5:

Action list	
Desk/computer	
Write last chapter (history assignment)	20th Apr
Complete Internet search (literature survey)	22nd Apr
Type up project aims and objectives	24th Apr
Read 'Aims and objectives' to Jim	25th Apr
Write plan for literature survey contents page	25th Apr
Email supervisor re: aims and objectives	27th Apr
Library	
Get choir music	23rd Apr
Check references for history assignment	23rd Apr
Check journal section for literature survey	23rd Apr
Home	
Put choir music in folders	24th Apr
Select colour scheme for spare room	5th May
Phonecalls	
Bus company (cheap tickets for A. Eve)	3rd May
Invite friends for painting party	10th May
Anywhere	
Choose music (choir)	19th Apr
Brainstorm project aims and objectives	22nd Apr
Read initial report specification	25th Apr
Sketch basic sections of initial report	27th Apr
Proofread history report	30th Apr
Shopping	
Paint for spare room	7th May

Figure 2.5 Example action list

Notice the following features of the example action list.

- The deadlines have been listed along with the action. This is so that you are aware of the relative urgency of each action. In fact, the actions are arranged in date order within each category. You do not have to do it like this, but it gives you some sense of which need completing before others. You may prefer to mark up deadlines in a different way (e.g. [by Friday], or [ideally during week 6]) – whatever you are most comfortable and familiar with.
- The titles of each action have been changed so that it makes sense in the new context. Where 'Write last chapter' had made perfect sense in the row of the project list called 'History assignment', when it is isolated under the 'Desk' heading on the action list, it requires a reminder that this is about the history assignment, so it becomes, 'Write last chapter (history assignment)'. Likewise, 'Check references in library' (on the project list) turns into a 'Library' action entry called, 'Check references for history assignment'.*
- The category 'Anywhere' refers to those paper-based tasks that could be done at home or on the bus, etc., in that they just need reading and possibly marking up with a pen.
- Not all the actions from the project list are brought across. Some are so date-specific that they should be entered onto the calendar to ensure that they are done on a certain time on a given day. For example, the History assignment's 'Take to departmental office' would become a calendar/diary entry called 'Take history assignment to departmental office'.

---

* This changing of context takes some getting used to. Have you ever done something like this? You and Jim are arranging to meet for lunch. You say 'let us meet here next Monday at noon'. In your diary under the following Monday you write, 'meet here next Monday at noon' because those are the words ringing around your head. When next Monday arrives, you look at your diary and see, 'meet here next Monday at noon'. But *who* were you meant to meet? And *where*? What you should have written was '12:00 – meet Jim for lunch in Library snack bar'. In general, when you write a note to yourself (or an entry in your time management system) you need to use words and information that will be useful to you *when you wish to look at it*.

Daily planner

Even though the action list has broken down all the complex tasks of your life into a series of simpler actions to be carried out, it is still rather distracting on a day-to-day basis. It includes reminders of many things that do not necessarily have to be done 'today'. So, some people like to produce a daily planner, which incorporates the calendar events for the day, and the actions which *have to be* carried out, and those which *could be*.

Other people see the daily planner as an unnecessary step; as all the information the Worker needs is on the calendar and in the action list. You must choose for yourself whether or not to use it. The biggest advantage of preparing the daily planner is that this gives you a managerial review at the end of one day, or the start of the next. It is a common experience to come to the end of each day and find that planning the next day is a very good way of 'closing' the day, leaving yourself mentally free for the evening.

What follows (in Figure 2.6) is an example daily planner, showing a hypothetical day in the life of someone who owns the project and actions lists above. Let us examine some of its features:

- There are not many appointments for this day, therefore it is up to the Worker to select which tasks to do and when. Two of the actions are marked in *italics* as they are overdue or are due today.
- Some people prefer to mark up their daily planner with specific times in which they plan to do their actions (e.g. putting 08:30–10:00 'Write last chapter'). There are advantages and disadvantages to this approach. The advantage of this is that you will probably use that allocated time for that purpose (which may be good for this chapter-writing task as it really does need to be done today). The disadvantages are that you block out all your time in advance, which makes it difficult to be more flexible in your approach to time, as things can change on an hour-by-hour basis. Also, if you schedule a fixed time, you are quite likely to spend that amount of time doing it. This can be a good or a bad thing, depending on the accuracy of your estimation of the time the task will take.
- There is a space in the bottom-right corner marked 'Incoming'. This is where you write down anything which needs to be

Daily planner	
Date: **Monday 20th April**	**Action list**
	Desk/computer
08:00	*Write last chapter (history assignment)* 20th Apr
08:30	Complete Internet search (literature
09:00	survey) 22nd Apr
09:30	
10:00 Supervision	**Home**
10:30 –	Put choir music in folders 24th Apr
11:00	
11:30	**Library**
12:00 meet Jim for lunch	Get choir music 23rd Apr
(Library snack bar)	Check references for history assignment 23rd Apr
13:00	Check journal section for literature
13:30	survey 23rd Apr
14:00	
14:30	**Anywhere**
15:00	*Choose music (choir)* *19th Apr*
15:30	Brainstorm project aims and objectives 22nd Apr
16:00	
16:30	**Shopping**
17:00	
Evening:	**Incoming**

Figure 2.6 Example daily planner

processed by your time management system. It could be an action you have just said 'yes' to (but which has not yet been put onto the action list, or which turned into a more complex task and was therefore entered into the project list), or an idea to investigate, or a date to put in your calendar which is not yet to hand. In other words 'Incoming' is a section where the Worker can write down anything that needs to be seen and processed by the Manager.

Using the four tools

It is important that you use the above tools (or your own version of them), and that you are *not* tempted by the alternative of using your memory as a time management tool. Around the world the following scenario regularly takes place when a supervisor is arranging the next meeting with his or her student:

Supervisor: [Looking at calendar on the computer] Er, how about 10.15 next Friday?
Student: [Not looking anywhere] Yes – that's fine.
Supervisor: [Knowing how complicated life is] Are you sure that's OK?
Student: Yes – no problem.
Supervisor: [Knowing how bad his own memory is] Aren't you going to write that down?
Student: No, that's fine. See you next week.
1 week later
Supervisor: [Getting on with work in office, waiting for student who never turned up]
Student: [Sitting in another lecture which hadn't been written down, and completely unaware that a meeting with their supervisor had been missed]

Your brain is bad at remembering *when* things should happen compared to a calendar (whose only job in life is to store reminders of events). It is awful at remembering *what* to work on because it is clouded by emotion and energy levels, neither of which are completely predictable. However when you are looking at a pre-prepared action list, you can use your emotions and current energy states to choose the most appropriate action from your list. It is bad for your psychological state of mind to have lots of 'actions' (unresolved activity) stored in your brain.

The four tools described above define the *interface* between the Manager and the Worker. The Manager keeps the project list and calendar up to date and uses them to prepare the action list and the daily planner for the Worker. The Worker, therefore, only has to look at the daily planner (which shows what is scheduled for today).

You should hold a management meeting at the following times:

- With each major project event (whenever something new or unexpected occurs that is not covered by your current plans, or for each major scheduled event such as setting objectives, or completing a report).
- Every week. A weekly review of all your projects, and the updating of the action list, is necessary to keep all your four tools up to date.
- Every day (e.g. in the evening to prepare tomorrow's daily planning).

At each of these management events, you should take stock of where you are in each project, and what needs to be done next. Always ensure that you are checking things from your calendar and project list, and are making sensible choices about what to do next. Always keep the tools up to date, by adding appointments and deadlines to your calendar as soon as you know about them, and by adding new actions to your lists whenever you decide to say 'yes' to something. If it is a small action (e.g. photocopy a report) it can go straight onto your action list. If it is more complex (e.g. prepare a short talk), it is probably best to make a new entry in your project list, and begin the process of breaking it down into smaller actions and setting sub-deadlines.

Paper or computer

Each of the main time management tools (calendar, project list, action list and daily planner) can be purely paper-based, or they can be computerised, or can consist of a combination of both. This is something that you need to work out for yourself. Some people love using computers so much that they will be much better organised if they can use computers to hold all their lists and appointments. Others are much more comfortable with paper lists. Here are the basic issues you will have to consider when making a decision to use paper or computer.

- Computers are good for backing up information, but only if you have a system that works and you backup regularly. If you lose your paper diary/planner, how do you get the information back?
- Some people think better with a screen, mouse and keyboard, and others with a pen and paper.
- Portable computers can allow you to take a lot of information around with you, but they still tend to be slower than paper and pen (or voice recording) for inputting or recalling information.

All of the tools and techniques will be much more effective if you customise them for your own purposes. Design, print and copy your own forms based on the ideas discussed in this chapter, and start using them on a regular basis. It will probably take several weeks of refinement before they are truly suited to your needs, but most people find an increased sense of confidence and competence when they begin to use such a system.

Summary

In this chapter we have looked at a number of issues concerning the management of how you spend your time. We have noted that a number of time management methods already exist, and we can learn from what they have in common. However, it is important that you develop your *own* system. To help you get started we have discussed the four most important tools that will help your Manager keep track of all major events in your life, and to communicate the appropriate information to your Worker. These tools are the calendar, project list, action list and daily planner. Try using them as soon as possible, and refine them over time.

There is a specific type of time management that deals with the lifetime of a particular project and how all its sub-projects fit together within a schedule. We will look at this in more detail in Chapter 5. However, you cannot plan the detailed time-response of a project before you have worked out what the project is really all about. This is the subject of the next chapter – setting your aims and objectives.

Chapter 3

Your project's aims and objectives

Introduction

This chapter takes you through the vital task of setting and refining your project's aims and objectives. We start our look at the process from the point when you choose a project, and make it really yours. We then discuss how to form the project title, how to define aims, objectives, and a hierarchy of tasks, all of which will act as a guideline to the rest of your project. This chapter introduces several ideas for generating and managing creative ideas, and then communicating them to others in a clearly written proposal.

Selecting a project

At one point in time you did not have a project, and then some time later you are working on one. What happened in between? How did you get to 'own' this project? There are four basic ways for this to happen:

1   You are given a project (no choice).
2   You are given a choice of pre-defined projects.
3   You are given an example list of projects, but submit your own.
4   You set the entire scope of your own project.

In the following sections we will consider each one in turn.

You are given a project (no choice)

This is typically called an *assignment* because it is a project that is assigned to you, and that you must carry out to a given specification.

Even though you have no choice of which project to do, you soon realise that there are many ways to make this project your own. What you are given is a broad outline, and you still have a great deal of choice about the particular focus, the flow, the central argument, the detailed implementation, the final conclusions, and the writing style. With an assignment, there is usually no need for an interim report, and you simply hand in your final work.

You are given a choice of pre-defined projects

Many undergraduate projects take the form of a set of project suggestions that have come from individual supervisors, and are often related to the courses they teach, or their own research topics. You may then be asked to submit your choice of project (or maybe your first, second and third preference).

It is important for you to make a shortlist of your favoured topics as soon as possible, and then ask for a meeting with each potential supervisor. At this meeting you should aim to establish how much of the project is prescribed (i.e. has the supervisor got a specific job which needs to be done?), and how much is open to negotiation. Many supervisors actively encourage your own ideas at this stage, and this can be an important conversation in establishing a joint 'picture' of what the project focus will be. With these sorts of projects, you will probably be asked to submit an initial project report, early on in the process, to give a statement of your topic area and aims. This chapter will help you to focus your ideas, and thus enable you to write this report.

You are given an example list of projects, but submit your own

If you are doing a Masters-level project, you may well be expected to form your own definition of the project. Your starting-point is often a list of topics that are available (as above, often linked to the teaching or research topics of particular staff members), and from which you need to develop your own ideas. Ideally, these should be developed in consultation with a potential supervisor, and culminate in the submission of a project proposal. This proposal needs to clearly outline the topic you are working on, the specific aim(s) of the project, and the objectives that you propose to undertake. It may also be advisable to include a short initial survey of the literature associated with your topic (and this will be considered further in Chapter 4).

You set the entire scope of your own project

At doctoral level, the responsibility falls almost entirely to you for setting the scope of your project, and for ensuring that it represents novel work that pushes forward research in your subject area. Although you will be associated with a supervisor, you will probably see them less frequently than for projects undertaken earlier in the education system. This is primarily because it is entirely *your* project; you are not following a well-charted course, but are instead experimenting with the boundaries of knowledge in your particular subject area. It is therefore vital when making an application for doctoral work to justify why this work needs to be done, why it is novel, and how it relates to the existing knowledge base. It would not be out of place for you to construct your aims and objectives, as this chapter outlines, when *applying* for a PhD, as this will be your first task if you are accepted, and will demonstrate clearly to a potential supervisor that you have an outline plan of what you would like to do.

Whichever type of project you are undertaking, it is important to make the proposal really *yours*. Do not use words that the supervisor used if you do not understand them. Rephrase the project brief so that you can clearly tell anyone what your project is all about, and why you are doing it.

Setting the overall focus

The opposite of having a clear focus is being vague about what you are doing. Imagine for a moment that you were going on a car journey. How many of you would set out on such a journey without knowing where you were going? How would you know where to turn the wheel on a moment-by-moment basis? Yet this is what many students do, and they sustain this state for an amazingly long time by keeping 'busy' – which is analogous to driving around very fast without establishing where you are heading. Pushing this analogy a bit further – would it not be rather strange to stop and ask directions:

Driver: Excuse me, I'm lost.
Police Officer: OK, where are you going?

Driver: I've no idea, but I'd still like you to tell me how to get there.

Even though this is a rather ludicrous conversation, many students expect their supervisor to play the role of the police officer. Run the conversation again, once the goal has been set, and see how differently it turns out:

Driver: Excuse me, I'm lost.
Police Officer: OK, where are you going?
Driver: I need to find a supermarket, but I'm new to the area.
Police Officer: Well, I think there are two main ones you could go to. I'd suggest going over the bridge to the next village. Turn right onto the ring-road and you'll find a superstore on your left. If you get lost, ask again for directions at the shop in the village . . .

In other words, once you have set your goal you can ask for help, and you can work at getting there.

Therefore, you need to determine *what your subject area is*, and you should develop some idea of *what you are trying to achieve*.

As soon as possible practise explaining your topic and goal to as many people as will listen to you. If a friend (who is not studying your subject) asks you about your project, try to reply using everyday words. Sometimes this can help to cement the ideas in your own mind, and to help you feel comfortable with your project. However, you should also have some deep and detailed discussions with people who are more familiar with your subject area. This should be the topic of an early conversation with your supervisor, or another member of staff who understands the subject, or indeed your fellow students who have trained with you, but are now doing other projects.

At this early stage, you should allow yourself permission to dream. Rather than restricting yourself by saying, 'I've only got four months, and I'm new to the subject; what can I possibly do in that time?', think more like this: 'If my resources were unlimited, what would I like to achieve in an ideal project?' Permit yourself to think of a breakthrough in your particular area. Try to visualise what a great outcome for your project might be. A really good test of a worthwhile project is to ask, 'How will the world be different when I have completed this project?'

After a session of dreaming, you will of course need to come back to reality, and ask questions such as:

- How many hours in total do I have for this project?
- How much training do I need before I can really start making progress?
- How much equipment and support are available in my department?
- Where might I need to look for other resources?

An extremely powerful recipe for a successful project is:

- know your topic
- identify a dream of what you could do
- have a clear idea of the limitations associated with the project.

Techniques for generating ideas

In the early stages of your project, you may find it quite difficult to clearly identify your topic, let alone come up with an excellent idea for taking the subject area forward. In this section we will outline a few methods for getting your brain working in a creative mode.

Mind-mapping

An increasingly popular way of managing creative thinking is to generate a mind-map. This is essentially a method for recording ideas and associations that your brain comes up with, without restricting the order in which you have ideas. Tony Buzan popularised the idea in the 1980s (Buzan and Buzan, 1993), and nowadays there is even software available to help you manage the process. Figure 3.1 shows an example mind-map, made on the computer program *MindManager* (Mindjet, 2004) showing part of this chapter's structure. However, whether you work better on paper or computer, the basic process is the same.

To use mind-mapping to generate some project ideas, start in the middle of the page with something that represents the topic of your project. It could be a picture that portrays the concept, or the name of the topic, or if you are really stuck – just the word 'Project'. Now each time you have an idea, draw a line radiating out from the centre, and write on top of the line a brief summary of the idea.

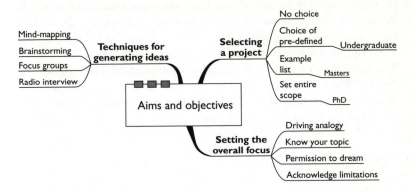

Figure 3.1 A mind-map showing a draft structure for part of this chapter

You may find that this sparks off a related idea, which you can attach to the previous idea (like a branch off a tree-trunk). On the other hand you may find you have a completely new idea (this is very common), so start a new line in a different direction, radiating from the centre. You can add diagrams where appropriate, and build this up in whatever way you like. Many mind-mappers find that using pens of different colours helps the ideas to flow.

People new to mind-mapping often find that after a slow start, they are generating ideas faster than they can write them down. A mind-map is often quite a good way of explaining a complex idea to someone else, as they can see the structure of your thoughts, and the relationships between them. Some people use mind-maps in their reports to summarise complex ideas. Still others go on to use them as a wonderfully engaging way to take notes in lectures or meetings. If you have never made a mind-map, please have a go during this project period; you may just discover an invaluable tool.

Sometimes (especially when thinking about the particular focus of your project) you may find that there are several clusters of ideas. This is sometimes referred to as a 'Topic Web', and shows your discovery of the relationships between the different aspects of your subject area.

Brainstorming

Mind-mapping is a technique for writing down ideas as they occur to you. The general process of coming up with ideas has often been referred to as brainstorming. This is simply a state of mind where you give yourself permission to have ideas *without judging them*. What people have found is that if you generate many ideas, then some of them will be good. However, if you start by restrictively looking for 'good ideas' then there are not many to be found. Brainstorming can be a solo activity, or something you can do in a group. When there is more than one person present, you can take turns in asking questions and jotting them down, or have competitions for the most ideas, or anything to get you thinking.

Focus groups

A wonderful way of working is to team up with people who are also studying in your subject area, or at least a topic that has something in common with yours. It is even better if these are fellow students who understand exactly what you are going through because they are at the same stage in their project. Ask critical questions of each other, for example:

'What exactly *is* your topic then?'

'Surely that's been done before. What's different about what *you* are doing?'

'How does that relate to the topic?'

'Why would you want to do that?'

'OK, I see what you are saying, but how would you explain this to someone who's *not* done our course?'

Read each other's reports, plans and jottings. Make sure that you understand what each other is saying, and what you have each written. Pretend to be examiners for each other. This can be fun, and a bit scary, but you will begin to respond to critical questions, and to prepare for explaining and justifying your project (more on this in Chapter 9). A good focus group can work together successfully throughout the project period and provide a level of everyday support which is mutually beneficial.

Radio interview technique

A particularly useful technique for formulating your project topic is to put yourself under imaginary pressure to explain it well. The following is a transcript of a conversation I have often had with my new students.

Me: OK, let's talk about your project. What do you think the focus is?

Student: Well [*sigh*] I don't really know. I've been thinking about it, but it's all rather complicated . . .

Me: [Holding an imaginary microphone under the student's chin] Hi, I'm from the local radio station. We're doing a feature on the university, and what students are studying these days. Tell me in 30 seconds what you are looking into and why. OK? Go . . .

Student: OK, I'm doing a project on computer interfaces. Typically these are not very good for real-time tasks, and I'm trying to find ways to improve this situation, particularly for people with limited movement.

Very often students are impressed with the eloquence of their spontaneous replies, and they reply with, 'Hold on a minute, I need to write this down'. It seems as if a bit of artificial pressure can bring ideas from the subconscious out into the open. Students are often surprised that deep down they knew all along what they were doing. We often use this as a starting-point for writing down the topic of study, and from there we will come up with the title, and the aims and objectives.

Title, aims and objectives

These three attributes of your project are perhaps the most important things to establish early on. The title announces to the world (and to yourself!) what you are studying and what you are doing. The aims define what you are trying to achieve. The objectives describe the main steps you plan to take to achieve the aims. You can always come back and define these later, but an early statement of them gives you the direction and focus you need to begin with.

Title

It is good practice to spend some time coming up with a working title for your project, as this will provide a sense of focus and direction to your work. The time you spend on this task is an investment, because it forces you to think about the work you plan to do. A good title should define the *topic area* you are working in and a hint of what you are going to *do* about it.

Here are some example titles that do both of these:

A prototype user-interface for helping people with disabilities to make music.

An investigation into the causes of the common cold.

Repetitive structures: a critical study of minimalism in the operas of Philip Glass.

The above titles also share another helpful feature – they should, where possible, make sense to the person in the street. Titles such as 'Categorisation of multiple spin techniques in the diomorphine substructure using electrolaryngographically derived surface textures' may appear impressive, but to the average person it is almost as if they are nonsense. (I'll leave it to you to work out if this title is a real one or not!) Typical doctoral titles simply state the subject area (e.g. Complex real-time user interfaces) as they are meant to be an in-depth study on a particular area. However, doctoral theses also should be reporting *novel work done* and so it is a good idea to reflect this in the title whenever possible.

Your title can evolve with the project. Think of it as a working statement of your chosen area of focus and activity. The title should lead directly on to your aims.

Aims

People are often confused by the labels 'aims' and 'objectives'. Very simply, the aims are statements of the things you want to *achieve* by the end of the project. Objectives describe *how to get to your aim* by listing the main stages you will need to undertake.

Let us assume that there is a single focused aim. Imagine you are being interviewed for a radio news bulletin, and someone asks you to complete the sentence:

'The main aim of my project is . . .'

or

'The thing that I want to have done by the end of the project is . . .'

Taking some of the examples mentioned in the 'Title' section above, you should then come up with phrases like this:

- To design and build a prototype user-interface to help people with physical disabilities to make music in non-real-time using computers.
- To investigate the causes of the common cold, considering specifically the airborne transmission of viruses from one human to another.
- To critically examine the operas of Philip Glass in comparison to other twentieth-century 'minimalist' composers; focusing on the precise methods for developing repetitive musical structures.

Do not worry if your aim looks very much like your title; this probably shows that your title is good. However, the aim is typically longer than the title, and gives a little more detail of what you want to deliver at the end of the project. If your aim is very long, with many clauses such as, 'To do . . . and to do . . . and also . . .' then you probably have a *list* of aims. Try listing them separately and see what they look like.

Once you have defined your aim(s) the next process is to bring your project to life with a list of objectives.

Objectives

Put at their simplest, *objectives* are the steps that you need to carry out in order to reach your aim. There are normally many objectives, which exist as an ordered sequence of action phrases. In other words, many 'objectives' will be a numbered list of sentence fragments such as, 'To analyse the existing work in this topic'.

There are different ways of setting objectives, but a good way to start is to look at your stated 'aim' and ask yourself, 'If I'm going to achieve this aim, what will I have to do?'

You can even use worry and panic to your own advantage here! For example, if you are feeling worried that you are not going to be able to do achieve much in this project, then allow your Worker to have a conversation with your Manager (but make sure nobody is watching!). Let us eavesdrop on a typical conversation, using the first of the project examples mentioned above.

Worker: I don't know how I'm going to achieve my aim.

Manager: What *is* your stated aim?

Worker: [Reads] 'To design and build a prototype user-interface to help people with physical disabilities to make music in non-real-time using computers.'

Manager: OK, good, but what worries you about this?

Worker: I don't want to re-invent the wheel.

Manager: Fine, so what do you need to do to make sure you don't re-invent the wheel?

Worker: Do something original!

Manager: OK, but exactly how will you ensure that it's original?

Worker: I'd better find out what already exists?

Manager: Good – write that down as objective number 1.

Worker: [Writes] 1. Find out what already exists.

Manager: Now if you read that objective out of context, would it make sense to someone?

Worker: [Reads] '1. Find out what already exists.' Mmm – sounds like I'm trying to survey the whole of creation. OK, so how about '1. Survey literature and web to establish existing methods of making music on computers for people with limited movement'?

Manager: Sounds good. So what would you do after that?

Worker: I'd have to design my own original system.

Manager: What would you need to do to get started on that right now?

Worker: Well, I'd have to work out what was *missing* from the existing work. Oh, yes, I suppose I could ask people working in this area what they would like to see invented.

Manager: OK, sounds good. Could you write that down as number 2?

Worker: '2. Contact people working in this area with a questionnaire'?

Manager: and . . . ?

Worker: Then analyse the questionnaire and decide on an original feature.

Manager: Right. Then what? Is the project finished yet?

Worker: No, nothing's built yet. And that's what really worries me; my programming skills are not very good.

Manager: So what could you put down as an objective?
Worker: Get better programming skills?
Manager: Mmm – yes, but how?
Worker: OK – I see '3. Revise computer programming course; highlighting particular coding problems needed for the novel interface'.
And so on.

This conversation would continue for some time, but I hope you can see the general idea. By simply identifying your tasks (and acknowledging your worries and weaknesses along the way) you begin to build up a set of activities that need to be done. You should revise your objectives and talk them through with your supervisor and focus group. The above example, when completed, looked like this:

Title:
A prototype user-interface for helping people with disabilities to make music.

Aim:
To design and build a prototype user-interface to help people with physical disabilities to make music in non-real-time using computers.

Objectives:
1   Survey literature and web to establish existing methods of making music on computers for people with limited movement.
2   Produce and analyse a questionnaire aimed at practitioners in the fields of music, computers and disability to find out what new equipment is needed.
3   Draw up a design specification for the novel interface.
4   Identify most suitable programming language: revise main feature of the language.
5   Plan necessary hardware; order components and book workshop time.
6   Build the hardware and write the software.
7   Test completed prototype system in the lab, then with a local special school.

If you are still stuck with your objectives, you may wish to think about whether they make sense from the point of view of the flow of time. Does the first objective lead naturally into the second? Is there something missing? Can the two tasks be run concurrently, or does one need to be completed before the next one begins?

When you have settled on your working objectives, it is important to think about breaking them down even further – until they become items that your Worker can easily carry out without worrying too much about them.

Turning objectives into tasks

The plan you have written down can change. You have the right to change it; it is your project. But for now, at least you have a plan. Something magical begins happening now in your brain. Because you have identified a series of objectives, you will find that you begin applying the questioning process to *each* of the above objectives.

Taking each of the objectives in turn (and forgetting temporarily about the rest) take yourself through the process of asking, 'Exactly what do you mean by that'? If you do not know the answer – write down at least how you propose to find out (ask your supervisor, email an expert, phone up a local contact, brainstorm the idea with your fellow students, do a web-search, etc.). The human brain has been shown to work well with lists of seven items or fewer! So, try to limit the number of objectives to no more than seven, then also limit the number of sub-objectives. We seem to be able to focus on a *sub*-list of items, as long as they are sensibly grouped together. So, keep on working on your objectives, and sub-objectives, until you have quite a detailed plan of what to do.

Taking our example above, we might come up with something like this (showing here how objective no. 1 has been broken down):

1   Survey literature and web to establish existing methods of making music on computers for people with limited movement.
   1.1   Brainstorm main subject areas to establish keywords
      1.1.1   Jot down initial ideas
      1.1.2   Schedule a focus group session to discuss this
      1.1.3   Organise a supervision to discuss ideas
      1.1.4   Run ideas past my contact at the local special school
   1.2   Visit library to identify main journals and books in the subject
      1.2.1   Log on to library computer and perform search
      1.2.2   Book appointment with subject librarian

1.2.3   Note down relevant journals
1.2.4   Skimp-read all relevant journals and books from 1990
1.2.5   Photocopy relevant articles
1.2.6   Borrow appropriate books
1.2.7   Schedule time to read copied articles and books
1.3   Web-search on the topics identified in the brainstorm
1.3.1   Fix amount of time willing to spend on this task
1.3.2   Follow-up web links from photocopied journals
1.4   Build up a database of contacts (including web-based newsgroups)
1.4.1   List all author contacts from journals and books
1.4.2   Ask supervisor for contacts and recommendations
1.4.3   Expand this list – with further brainstorming
1.5   Write up literature survey
1.5.1   Check suggested length/detail required with supervisor
1.5.2   Read previously submitted surveys (even in unrelated topics)
1.5.3   Decide on main structure; check with focus group
1.5.4   Create reference list from journals, books, web, etc.
1.5.5   Schedule writing of the entire chapter
2   Produce and analyse a questionnaire aimed at practitioners in the field of music, computers and disability.
And so on.

I hope that you can see from this that the art of creating a detailed project plan involves thinking about things in gradually greater detail. You need to find your own methods of fooling your brain that there is only one particular sub-topic that you are thinking about at the moment – and usually it will reward you by coming up with questions, break-downs, ideas and solutions *at that level*. However, if you try to address the whole picture, it is simply too complicated and you may get confused.

To summarise:

- write down what you *know*;
- list what you *do not* know yet but need to;
- work on one sub-section and break it down into further sub-topics.

The project proposal

Some projects require you to write an initial report in the early stages. Even if this is not a requirement at your place of study, it is strongly recommended that you write one. This report becomes the first statement of what the project means to *you*. It shows to your tutor not only that you understand the topic, but that you have a plan and some idea of how to bring it to life.

For doctoral studies (and some Masters-by-Research courses) this proposal needs to be presented up-front (i.e. *before* you are accepted onto the course because you are expected to be responsible for running your own research).

Whichever level you are working at, you should aim to write a report (a few pages long) that states your agreed title, aims and objectives. Sometimes this is enough, as it says what focus area you have agreed on, and what you plan to do about it. However, you may also want to add some background or introductory material if you feel that some explanation is needed *before* the aim makes proper sense.

For some initial reports you are given more time, and you may wish to also include a literature survey (see Chapter 4 for more details), and a time-plan (see Chapter 5).

So, whichever format you choose, you should aim at writing a short report that clearly explains what your project is, and what you are going to do about it. Ask for feedback from your supervisor, because the earlier you can establish a mutually acceptable writing style the easier it will be to write your final report.

Summary

We have considered how to select a project, and to make it your own. By the process of managing your ideas, and gradually refining them, you will arrive at a statement of your understanding of the project. This should describe both the topic area and the actions you hope to achieve within that area.

- The *title* summarises the whole statement very briefly.
- The *aim* states clearly what you hope to achieve.
- The *objectives* provide an ordered list of activities you intend to carry out to achieve the aim.

- The *tasks* are derived by gradually breaking down the objectives into more manageable chunks.

Finally, all of the above is put down on paper in the form of an initial report, which is your first statement to the world that you now *own* this project.

In the next chapter we look at how to write a literature survey, then in Chapter 5 we consider how to take the above plan as a starting-point, and use it to embark upon a successful project.

Chapter 4

The literature survey

Introduction

This chapter discusses the purpose of a *literature survey*, and then takes you through the task of carrying it out and writing it up. Whilst this is not a feature of every project, it is certainly an important milestone in many higher degrees, and is a key feature of all research.

The importance of setting your work in context

Before embarking upon any big task in life it is sensible to ask (and then answer) the following questions:

- Has anyone else already done this?
- Has anyone done something similar from which I can learn?
- Is anyone working on this, or something similar, at the moment?
- What am I doing, therefore, that is unique?

These questions are particularly relevant to a research project, and the higher up the education system you go the more important they become. Typically, for school projects you simply need to demonstrate that you can *do* what you have been asked to do, although it shows enterprise to comment on what other things have been done. For lower-level undergraduate project work, you need to show competence in the *techniques* being studied, and that you can *manage* a project. However, a survey of existing techniques and applications can set the context for your work and show initiative.

For higher-level undergraduate projects and Masters work you need to confirm that you know *where your work fits in* with other similar work around the world and in the literature, and that your work is *informed* by this research. For doctoral level work your research needs to be so thorough that you can prove the *novelty* of your work.

So let us look at how you can answer these four important questions that will set the context for your work.

What has been done?

To answer the question, 'Has anyone else already done this?' we can do only two things:

1   Find out what has been *written* about the topic. In the next section we will compare some of the common ways of getting hold of this sort of information.
2   *Ask* someone knowledgeable about the topic. In Chapter 6, we will look at some guidelines for interacting with other people.

However, before you do either of these things, you need to have a good idea of what your 'topic' is, or you won't know where to look or what to ask. If you have worked through the book up to this point, then you should have developed a title, an overall aim and some supporting objectives, which define in some detail what you think you would like to do.

You can take these as a starting point for defining your project topics. Usually your title will contain a few important keywords. Revisit Chapter 3, especially the section 'Setting the overall focus' to refresh your perspective on your topic.

You may well be asked for your literature survey *before* you have had a chance to develop your project plan in detail. There is a lot of sense to this approach, because it forces you to examine 'what is out there' before you commit large amounts of time working out the details of what you are going to do. It also helps you to work more in Manager mode, by examining existing work before embarking upon your own work. A further advantage is that a written literature survey will usually form an important part of your final project report, and this will give you a good head start on the report at an early stage of the project (more on this in Chapter 8).

Chapter 3 contained two sections that took you through the planning of a literature survey as an example of how to plan. You may wish to revisit these sections before moving on. In the 'Objectives' section, we saw how your desire to do something original would naturally lead to an investigation of the literature, and consequently the search for this literature became the first major objective. In the section 'Turning objectives into tasks', we worked out a plan for the literature survey that was composed of many smaller tasks, each of which is easily handled.

You have established that you need to discover what has been previously written in your topic area. Let us now examine the different potential sources of the information you are looking for.

Different types of information source

This section considers the variety of forms that information comes in, and is intended as a sort of 'travel guide' to the different media, with things to do and areas to beware of. We will look at the various types of media, and discuss the advantages and disadvantages of each. Remember that a good literature survey is *not* just a list of references (or a concatenation of quotes). Instead, it should consist of a carefully reasoned argument that references other people's work, analyses it, comments on it, introduces your own ideas, and leads up to your main project work.

Figure 4.1 shows a list of publication types and compares their principal features. Books are considered very reliable because of the editing process, but they traditionally take a long time to produce and so cannot contain the latest information in a rapidly changing field. Advertising is clearly up to date, but cannot be

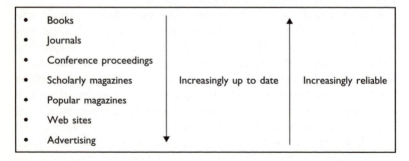

- Books
- Journals
- Conference proceedings
- Scholarly magazines   Increasingly up to date   Increasingly reliable
- Popular magazines
- Web sites
- Advertising

Figure 4.1 Some different media types and the reliability trade-off

considered reliable as an independent opinion. Of course, this list is a gross generalisation (for instance some books may well be unreliable, and there is a lot to be learned from advertising), but you need to be aware from the start that just because something is written does not mean that it is correct. In a literature survey, the reader will want to know what you *think* of each piece of work that you reference.

In the following sections we consider each of these media types in turn, and what we can learn from each one.

Books

Typically books take a long time to complete, and have been through many processes of review. This affects the content, and gives time for the material to be considered, revised and checked. Books are often more accessible to the reader than journals and magazines (which tend to use a lot of terminology that requires specialist knowledge). But be aware that because of the long preparation time, books cannot easily comment on the latest developments, and so are often best used to 'set the scene' for your later reading from more up-to-date publications.

There is usually a strict editorial process on the quality of a book, but there is one danger that you must consider. Whereas journals and magazines tend to sell via a reasonably steady subscription (to a fixed set of readers), books are usually sold individually via bookshops, and author and publisher will gain financially for every copy sold. Thus, it is possible that a book could be sensationalised in some way to enhance the sales. This is more likely to happen in some subjects than with others, so be careful when considering the reliability of a book.

As a student doing a literature review, start with any appropriate book lists found in your syllabus, or given to you by your supervisor. Next, you should be acquainted with your library. Computers are wonderful tools, but the danger is that they can trawl up a huge amount of information of unknown quality, often dependent on the keywords you type into a search engine. In a library, you can locate the section for your subject, and just browse through a whole variety of books that have been classified as being relevant to that subject. Physically flicking through books, at a speed your brain is comfortable with, yields completely different insights about what information is relevant when compared with staring at a computer screen for hours. There are also subject librarians who can help you locate suitable books and journals, but you will first need to consider your research topic clearly before making an appointment.

Journals

Journals are subject-specific periodicals that are usually available in academic libraries and by subscription.* They are often considered the best compromise between reliability and speed of publication. Usually a journal has a strong emphasis on *peer reviewing*. This means that before a paper is published it has to go through a rigorous process of being read, analysed and commented on by (usually) more than one expert in the field of study. This ensures that the papers are acceptable to the current practitioners in the topic, but can make it quite hard to get radically new ideas published.

As such, journals are rather specialist publications, and can often feel quite inaccessible to someone outside the area, relying heavily on common knowledge in that area, without the need to continuously revisit the same explanatory material. Journals are generally well respected as sources of specialist information for research, primarily because of the reviewing process. They also encourage extensive cross-referencing, so rather than repeating other people's work, authors *quote* and *refer to* others' work. This makes them an excellent introduction to other references that you may not yet have come across. You can browse through journals in a library, or ask specialists in your subject area (e.g. your supervisor) if they particularly recommend certain papers to study.

Nowadays, much information about journals can be found on-line. Some journals (known as e-journals) only exist in electronic form, and so do not have a printed-paper copy. You still need to pay a subscription for many of these, so the information may not be 'free'. Most journals have a 'home-page' that contains lists of contents for each issue, often abstracts of every paper, and sometimes complete papers.

A useful method to get hold of a particular journal paper is to find out if it is available on-line. It could be that an individual author has made the paper available on his or her web site. Simply

---

* There are around ten thousand journals published in the UK alone.

type some keywords of the title (and possibly the first author's surname) into an Internet search engine, and patiently review the results – looking for the paper in question. This has the advantage that you may well discover other web pages or papers in this topic which share the same keywords, or indeed which *quote* the paper you are looking for.

Finally, there are various web sites that list journal citations, and often include a large repository of full papers and abstracts.*

Conferences

Conferences are gatherings of people (often academics or practitioners in a certain subject) where the main goals are to share ideas, hear presentations, and to meet people working in the same area. Speakers at a conference typically have more freedom than those writing for an academic journal. Often, presenters are expected to submit a paper, which is later published in a set of conference *proceedings*.

Sometimes conference proceedings are heavily refereed, in a similar way to journal papers. However, most conferences are considered to be reviewed a bit more 'freely' and a little less rigorously than journals. Some journals can take between one and two years to produce, whereas conferences are usually reporting work or ideas from the previous six months or so. Therefore the latest conference proceedings in a particular subject are a reasonably good overview of 'what is going on now' in that subject, but the papers do not carry quite as much 'weight' as a journal. Often you will see work presented at a conference and then later expanded into a journal paper.

Again, most conferences have their own web page, and it is becoming more common to see the full papers freely available on the conference web site.

Scholarly magazines

There are different sorts of magazine. Some are more like journals, in that there is quite a strong reviewing process. The main differences

---

* Since web-page addresses change, we are not listing individual pages here. But go to a good Internet search engine and try the following searches: 'journals (+ *your topic, e.g. electronics*)', 'journal citation', 'digital library'.

between journals and scholarly magazines is that journals are really intended for a *specific* audience and are rarely to be found in a shop, whereas magazines are written for a broader audience and sell most of their copies through newsagents.

The turnaround time for magazines is also much faster. This means that they can report in a more up-to-date manner in fast-changing subject areas, or produce very fast reports from conferences. However, this means that the depth of reviewing is usually less, and thus you have to read them with more caution. The very fact that they are written in a popular style (to make them accessible) means that they are rather restricted in their depth of technical or analytical detail.

Popular magazines

Popular magazines are designed to sell in bulk, and so are mainly found in newsagents. Often they are produced weekly, so the turn-around times for writing are very small. In many instances there is a very limited review process. This encourages people to write articles that will sell more magazines and which therefore have to be extremely accessible (and thus not technically deep). Quite often such magazines contain many tutorials, and news pages. The emphasis is more on training, entertainment, and advertising rather than scholarly research. Some articles may even be adverts in disguise. Therefore, while you may find some interesting ideas in magazines, beware of quoting them without following up the information further to discover its true source.

Web sites

As we have seen above, the Internet allows access to journals, conferences, and library catalogues, and so is nowadays regarded as an essential tool for research. However, with the freedom and accessibility of the Internet comes a warning. Anyone can write anything and put it on the Internet. Just because it is on the web, does not mean that it is correct. The Internet is unregulated by default, and so it is important that you evaluate the quality of review.

Positive things you should look out for include:

- Home pages of well-respected authors (these are often the source of many ideas and papers).

- A 'virtual community' which monitors or regulates the content of the site, and encourages discussion and sharing of ideas.
- Sites related to journals and conferences where a strong review process is known to take place.
- Sites that primarily give links to other information (portals). Again, weigh up who is providing the information and what their motives are for doing so.

For all other sites beware that you may be reading:

- advertising material (see next section);
- spoof material (the Internet is rife with jokes and made-up stuff);
- interesting material that has simply not been tested by the community.

Advertising

Advertisements are intended to make you buy something, or to promote a particular ideology. They are not there to provide you with a carefully considered independent point of view. Be *very* wary of quoting advertising. It is often written in a certain style (intended to manipulate) and this sits extremely uncomfortably in a report that is meant to be objectively surveying the area.

Imagine the following extract from your report on the topic of computer software used in graphics, specifically drawing.

> There are many programs available for artists, but the one to be used for this project is the Graph-o-Pad 3 by SuperDuperDraw Systems:
>
> '*Graph-o-pad 3 is the only drawing package you will ever need. Years ahead of its competition, this amazing package will allow your creativity to flow, enabling you to produce stunning artwork admired by all your friends*' [SuperDuperDraw web site, 2004]
>
> Clearly, this is the best program to use. The project will allow artists to . . .

As a reader of such a report, surely you will not be convinced by such an argument, which amounts to, 'I chose this system because I was brainwashed by an advert'?

Learning from other people

In the section above we have considered some of the many sources of written information for your literature survey. However, never underestimate what knowledge and advice might be lurking in the heads of people around you.

Talking about your project

At the risk of becoming a project bore, do try to talk to as many people as possible about your project and *listen* to what they say. These could be fellow students on your course, your housemates (maybe at the same educational institution, but studying different subjects), non-student friends, or relatives. If people cannot understand what you are trying to do, then work harder at finding an explanation; this will help you when it comes to refining your aims and writing the report. However, quite often you will receive some very interesting ideas, some of which would never have come from an expert in your area!

Supervisor

We will discuss the role of your supervisor in Chapter 6, but for now be aware that this single person will generally be able to guide you to the relevant texts faster than anyone else. However, do not be surprised if he or she does not just give you a reading list; they may want you to exercise your research skills by letting you look for yourself first. When you are happy with what you have found, your supervisor is an excellent person to be asked, 'Do you think I've missed anything?'

Focus group

Your project focus group (see previous chapter) should be an integral part of your literature review process. These are fellow students who are working in a similar area to you. The members of a focus group can work together to:

- *compare* lists of literature found;
- *discuss* the contents and relevance of the literature;
- ask each other questions to see if you *understand* what you have read.

Librarians

People who work with academic literature every day are great sources of advice on how to use a library and on what written material exists. Many libraries also employ subject specialists. These people know about the structure of the literature in certain topic areas, and may know much of its contents too. This does not mean they will automatically understand the aims or details of your project, but they are certainly worth talking to in order to get some guidance about where you should look.

Other experts

You may wish to contact some of the specialists around the world in your particular subject area. Please read Chapter 6 ('Communicating with others') carefully before doing this. There are many people doing research, and fewer experts, so they do not want to be inundated with requests for information. You should perhaps discuss with your supervisor which people might be most approachable.

Questionnaires

Another source of information is a carefully designed and distributed questionnaire. This can be particularly useful if you are trying to canvass opinion on a certain topic. The Internet has certainly made this sort of information gathering easier, as questionnaires can be sent and received by email. However, you get more of a personal touch if you use physical sheets of paper that are given to people. Again, refer to Chapter 6 for guidance about how best to communicate with other people who are already very busy.

Writing the literature survey

This section gives you some advice about how to write the literature survey.

Main aim

Let us be clear what you are trying to do by writing a literature survey. You are demonstrating that:

- you know what other work exists in your topic area;
- you have gathered and read some subject-specific material;
- you can analyse and comment on existing work;
- you know how your proposed work relates to the existing work;
- you understand to what extent your proposed work is unique.

Different approaches

There are many ways to write a literature survey:

- An *essay-based* approach is usually text-based, and tells a story, referring to other work along the way.
- A *bibliography-based* approach lists the literature found, and says something about each one.
- A *topic-based* approach divides up the literature you have found into certain topic areas that are related to your project.

A good literature survey (whatever the style) will have a good *flow of argument* and will *reference* other work in the area. The flow of argument is important because it shows that you understand what your project is about, and how the other work relates to it. The referencing is important because it shows what other work exists.

Arguing your case

The most important thing to remember when you are writing a literature survey is that *your opinions matter* to the person reading it. Therefore it is important that you apply a personal 'filter' to the material you discover. The literature survey is your selection of what is 'out there'. You are not trying to represent all the literature that might be vaguely related to your topic; instead you are crafting a story that leads up to your specific project focus.

A literature survey should take the reader from a 'general knowledge' of the area, to a specific, focused description of your project. You should comment on the work of others, feeling free to criticise it if you disagree. Most importantly, you should try to *balance* your ideas with the ideas of others.

Referencing

It is highly important that you reference someone else's work when:

- you *refer* to it (e.g. This is covered in the book by Hunt);
- you *quote* directly from it (e.g. Hunt says, 'It is highly important that you reference someone else's work');
- you *paraphrase* (re-word) it (e.g. referencing someone else's work is very important).

There are several possible styles of referencing, and you should talk to your supervisor about which one is preferred. Some educational establishments prescribe the format, others leave it open.

One method is to use footnotes like this,* but this can clutter up the bottom of a page, and does not automatically provide a complete ordered list of references.

Another method is to provide a simple number in square brackets for each reference like this [1]. This must be supported by a numbered list of references at the back of the report.

A very popular method is to include the first author's name and the publication date in brackets straight after the reference occurs, like this (Hunt, 2005). At the back of the report is a full list of references arranged alphabetically by first author, as shown in Figure 4.2.

This has a dual advantage:

1 It provides some in-line information about the reference (e.g. if you know about Hunt's 2005 work, then you need look no further and your reading is not interrupted).
2 The alphabetic list of references at the back of the report forms a useful summary of all the material you have found in an easily accessible form.

Appendix A: References

. . .

Hunt, A., *Your Research Project: How to Manage it*, 2005

. . .

Figure 4.2 Extract from alphabetic reference list at end of report

---

* Hunt, A., 'Your Research Project: How to Manage it', 2005.

Two books in particular cover the details of referencing research projects (Hunt, 2005), and (Berry, 2000). When writing a report 'It is highly important that you reference someone else's work' (Hunt, 2005), because this shows that you understand what other people have written. Establishing the correct format is important too.

> There are several possible styles of referencing, and you should talk to your supervisor about which one is preferred. Some educational establishments prescribe the format, others leave it open.
>
> (Hunt, 2005)

Hunt later describes the dangers of plagiarism, because it is the opposite of good referencing (Hunt, 2005).

Figure 4.2 An example section showing referring, quoting and paraphrasing

Using this method, Figure 4.3 shows some examples of referring, quoting and paraphrasing used together in a single (highly contrived) paragraph.

In reality, if you were talking about 'Hunt, 2005' a lot, you would not need to reference it every time – but you must show which material has come from other people.

Plagiarism

Plagiarism is the use of other people's material *without* properly referencing it. In effect, it is cheating by pretending that the words and ideas on the page are yours, whereas in reality they have come from somewhere else. Most places of higher education treat this as a very serious offence.

The sheer volume of information available on the Internet makes it very easy to cut and paste material into your report. If you mark it clearly, list where it comes from, and comment on it appropriately, then this is acceptable. However, many people try to construct their work by finding pieces of it elsewhere and bolting it together, hoping that it will form an essay.

Plagiarism is wrong for the following reasons:

- it shows a lack of thinking and processing;
- it is simply unfair to those whose words you have stolen;

- it will *not* show you in a good light when questioned further about the work;
- it does not show off your research skills.

This last point is important. If you find something relevant and quote it and comment on it – you have demonstrated your ability to find elusive information and analyse its content. If, on the other hand, you pass it off as your own words you simply show your proficiency at cheating. The effort required to disguise someone else's work as your own is much better applied towards proper referencing.

Concluding the survey

Make sure that you finish the survey with a positive statement of what you will be doing for the rest of your project, or at least what the focus of your study is. Try to summarise the literature you have found, and what you thought of it, then describe what *you* are going to be focusing on and why.

Summary

This chapter has looked at the important topic of finding out what else has been done in your topic area. We have considered the different sources of information available to you, and compared their reliability and timeliness. We have thought about how to write the literature survey, and have stressed the importance of properly referencing other people's work. With your literature survey complete, you should know how your particular project fits into the bigger scheme of things, and this should help you to focus on your own individual work with renewed enthusiasm.

Chapter 5

Working towards success

Introduction

Previous chapters have discussed how to manage yourself, and then how to produce a written statement of focus on your particular project, along with a plan of the major steps to fulfil that aim, and a survey of the existing work in your topic area. In this chapter we take the outline plan one stage further, by converting it into a document that precisely outlines how your achievements will be measured along the way, and how they will fit into the available time.

Project storyboarding

The concept of storyboarding comes from the film industry. Writers and directors need to have a very detailed outline of the story before they allocate resources to filming, locations, actors and crew. A typical film storyboard consists of a series of sketched drawings that show the key points of the action in a film or animation. This is not a frame-by-frame plan of every detail, just the important events that mark out the story of the film. Usually each drawing is on a small card, and these are pinned to a board for all to see, hence the term *storyboard*.

A similar concept can be used to help you to plan your project, by sketching out the main points of action that you anticipate in the project. There is one key difference between its use in the film industry and in project planning. A director knows that the film must eventually bring to life all the cards on the board (i.e. the story must conclude by the end of the film). In your project, however, you do not yet know how long it will take to do each section, so you cannot assume that you will complete all the sections *and* do everything well! The project storyboard instead allows you to think about all the things that *could* be done in your project, and to place them in a sensible order. This concept acknowledges that at some point you *will* run out of time. If you are working to a well-organised storyboard, you will have done your best to tackle items in a sensible order, and what is left incomplete becomes 'further work'.

The act of putting together a storyboard, therefore, can help you to build a coherent project plan. You may be worried about using such an idea because you are not yet confident about what the major components of the project are, and more importantly in what order they should be carried out. Yet, if you ask some simple questions, you will realise that you already possess a common-sense approach to the ordering of a project. Can you carry out the testing before you have built a prototype product? No – so this tells you that 'testing' needs to come after 'building'. Does design happen before building? Yes – so put it in its place.

Already with just those two 'obvious' questions we can make a start at producing a storyboard (see Figure 5.1).

This is so simple that it offers you nothing that you did not know before, but it *does* give you a written framework to explore, change and expand. After some more thought you might decide that rather than designing it all, *then* building it all, *then* testing it all, you may wish to split up the task into smaller chunks. You may also note that you need to do various things before you start designing. You might sum up with something like Figure 5.2.

Figure 5.1 First stages of a storyboard

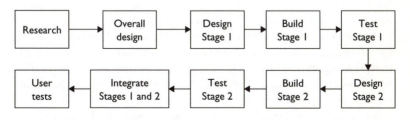

Figure 5.2 Evolution of the storyboard

Your project will probably look completely different to this, but all projects have stages and components – they are not a monolithic mass of work. The idea is to gradually flesh out the major components of the project, and place them in time order. Put as much information as you want into each box. If a box becomes too complex, this probably indicates that you need to convert it into several small boxes, each of which contains a simpler task. Eventually your storyboard may occupy several pages. Keep going until you are happy that the major project components are in the correct order.

One of the great benefits of the storyboard is that it allows you to discuss your detailed project flow with others. Because it puts onto paper your intended direction, you can get input from your focus group, your supervisor, or anyone who will listen to you. In fact, sometimes the non-specialist is the best person to ask, because they point out the obvious, as demonstrated by this semi-fictitious discussion of the storyboard in Figure 5.2:

Non-specialist:	So does your project *finish* with the User tests then?
Student:	Yes.
Non-specialist:	Really? – Don't you need to *analyse* the results?
Student:	Oh yes, I'd have to do *that*. [*Makes a mental note to enlarge the storyboard*]
Non-specialist:	What about writing it up? Do you have to do a write-up?
Student:	Of course.
Non-specialist:	Won't that take time? Could it go in here? [*Pointing to end of storyboard*]
Student:	Yes, of course. [*Another mental note*]
Non-specialist:	Why have you got *two* separate phases?
Student:	Er – well, I just *have*. [*Maybe some more thinking needs to be done.*]

Etc.

Every so often, pretend that *you* are someone who knows nothing about the project. Work through the storyboard from the beginning and jot down anything you think is wrong or missing. You may find that you add completely new sections that were simply forgotten in an earlier version.

Your final storyboard may end up being very detailed with forty or more steps, or it may be more of a high level representation of the project with a few items that outline the main phases. See what develops as the best choice for you and your project. Many people like to add images, or artists' impressions of what the project will look like at each stage, or a flowchart of how the interim project stage will work, or what it will contain.

Constructing the storyboard can be done in many ways:

- *Single sheet of paper:* Sketch out the whole flow on one page. This is simple and direct, but messy and time-wasting as soon as you need to make changes.
- *Cards:* Put each item on a postcard. These can be laid out on a table, or pinned to a board in the traditional manner. This provides a direct physical way of moving ideas around, but if you drop the set of cards you have lost your order!
- *Word-processor:* Simply type each item on a new line. You can use bullet-points or indentation to indicate a series of activities that make up an item.
- *Computer slideshow:* It may surprise you to know that one of the best tools for storyboarding is a standard presentation package* that allows you to prepare text and images in a slideshow to help you with your presentations. Each item on your storyboard goes on one slide. It is straightforward to type in text, and add graphics to illustrate a point. Using the 'slide overview' feature you can easily drag slides around to change the ordering. You can then print out the slide overview to give you a paper version of the storyboard with several slides (items) on each page. An added bonus is that you can put it into 'slide presentation' mode and make a simple presentation of your project idea to your focus group or supervisor, for example.

At the end of the storyboarding process, whichever method you have chosen, you should have a list of the most important phases and sub-phases of the project – in the right order. You have not promised to get them all done, and you have not said how long each phase will take, but you now have an overall plan that is visible to other people. Now we need to think about how to formalise and refine this plan, and a good way to start this process is by deciding what makes a successful project.

---

* Such as Microsoft PowerPoint

Criteria for success

It is important to think about how your progress can be monitored for several reasons:

- For your own peace of mind you need to know how the project is progressing towards your desired aim. If time is slipping, you can take corrective action, such as renegotiating the objectives with your supervisor.
- Other people (such as your supervisor or an external funding body) have a concern about how your work is progressing, so you need a way of reporting progress to them.
- It is the essence of the Manager's role to be aware of the current state of progress. Each time you have a review, you need to know where you *are*, in order to chart what needs to be *done* to get you to where you *want* to be. (Try reading that sentence again!)

Therefore it is advisable for a project to have a series of targets to meet. Later in this chapter we will consider in more detail the use of *time-planning* tools to set schedules, and to place targets on a measurable time-line. First of all, however, let us concentrate more on the factors you will use to judge your own progress. These factors are often referred to as *criteria for success*. In other words, how will you know that a chunk of your project has been achieved? What exactly would need to happen for you to 'tick off' one of your objectives as *done*? What makes a *successful* objective?

The distinction between an objective and a successful objective is subtle, so here is an example to clarify it. You may have written down an objective which says 'hand-in initial report'. Surely, therefore, if you hand in your initial report, you have achieved your objective? Well, not if it was handed in late. Not if it gets a 'fail' mark. Not if it does not help you to push the project forward. Maybe the criteria for success (the things that will make it an excellent report) are more complex. Here is an example list of criteria drawn up to define what a successful outcome of 'handing in the initial report' might look like:

- It is handed in on time (so, specify the deadline here).
- It meets the specification in your departmental handbook (specify the details here – e.g. number of pages, topics covered, referencing style).

- It is understandable in detail by a member of your focus group (specify how and when you will get a statement to that effect from a member of your group).
- The main aims are understandable by a non-expert person (specify how and when you will get such a statement from, for example, a member of your family).
- It gets a good mark (detail the criteria the marker – usually your supervisor – wants to see in an initial report, and schedule when you are going to proofread it prior to hand-in).
- It forms a 'springboard' for the work that is to follow (imagine yourself sitting down with your report, ready to work on the project – what sorts of things will be written down in order for the report to help you start work on the project details?).

Note how each of the above criteria will cause you to do *extra work* (read a handbook, note down specifications, proofread the document according to those specifications, schedule in time before the deadline to get feedback from focus group and others, etc.), and that is precisely the point! If you think about each of your objectives in detail, considering what would make them excellent, you will end up with more work to do. As a by-product, the whole thinking process supporting the project will become more rigorous. The characteristics that make a successful project will take place, simply because you have thought about them and have taken action to ensure they are done.

Compare the detailed criteria we just listed above with the original specification ('hand in initial report') and you get a good idea of the extra depth of thinking required to produce a smoothly running project.

Each of your main objectives should be analysed in this way; to establish what a 'successful outcome' would be like. Make sure that you schedule time in your calendar to check that the appropriate actions have been carried out.

Establishing key deliverables

Now that you have established what would constitute the successful completion of each objective, it is useful to list the *deliverables* that will occur as part of the work towards that objective. A deliverable is simply something concrete that is produced. Typical deliverables are as follows:

- reports (e.g. initial report, final report, literature survey, questionnaire summary, project web page);
- products (e.g. computer code, or a piece of hardware);
- presentations (e.g. concert performance, or talk to an audience).

In other words, a deliverable is typically something that is available to be shown or 'delivered' to other people. It is important to identify your deliverables, and build them into your schedule. Sometimes other people will give you fixed deadlines for certain deliverables, and for others you will need to set your own time-limits. We will discuss this in more detail in following sections.

From objectives to work packages

If you are dealing with a complex project, or a funding application, you may wish to formalise everything we have said so far by converting your objectives (outlined in Chapter 3) and your project storyboard into a series of *work packages*. What is presented here is simply a suggestion of how you might do this. You must customise the procedure to your own situation, but this is a reasonable model to start with.

We will assume that by now you have the following:

- a title
- a main aim
- an ordered list of objectives to reach that aim
- several levels of tasks which constitute each objective
- criteria for success for each objective
- a list of key deliverables associated with each objective
- some idea of the overall flow of the project (e.g. a storyboard).

Let us now produce a set of work packages – one for each objective – which will encapsulate the project work to be done in well-defined chunks. Each package will take the form outlined in Figure 5.3, but you are encouraged to edit this into something appropriate for your type of project.

- Each work package has a *number*, and it is useful to give it a *name* (such as 'research work', or 'implementation') to tag briefly its main function.

Work package *<number>* : *<name>*
Objective:
Overview:
Main tasks:
Key deliverables:
Criteria for success:

Figure 5.3 Template for a work package

- The *objective* is listed next, and this is taken directly from the major objective you have already written (see Chapter 3).
- This is followed by a descriptive *overview*, which outlines in plain language the focus of the work that needs to be done to carry out the objective.
- Next are listed the *main tasks*, which come from the breakdown of the objective into smaller, more precisely defined, work elements. You may list as many levels of your task hierarchy as you think are appropriate here.
- Finally, you list the *key deliverables* and the *criteria for success* associated with this objective.

Again, taking up the example we worked with in Chapter 3, we can now build up an example work package for the first objective (see Figure 5.4).

Note how in the *main tasks* section, not all the levels of task breakdown have been entered. How much detail you put in here is a matter of judgement, but your main concern should be that the workpage looks clear and coherent. Consider the lower-level sub-tasks of the type we developed in Chapter 3:

1.2.1 Log on to library computer and perform search
1.2.2 Book appointment with subject librarian
1.2.3 Note down relevant journals
1.2.4 Skimp-read all relevant journals and books from 1990
1.2.5 Photocopy relevant articles
1.2.6 Borrow appropriate books
1.2.7 Schedule time to read copied articles and books

Maybe if these were included, the impact of the work package would actually be reduced. Note the irony here – that putting in more

---

Work package 1: *Research*

Objective: Survey literature and web to establish existing methods of making music on computers for people with limited movement

Overview: This work package launches the project by investigating available literature, both in written form and on the web, and establishing a list of the main contacts that can be followed up later

Main tasks:

1.1   Brainstorm main subject areas to establish keywords
1.2   Visit library to identify main journals and books in the subject
1.3   Web search on the topics identified in the brainstorm
1.4   Build up a database of contacts (incl. web-based newsgroups)
1.5   Write up literature survey

Key deliverables:
* Database of contacts
* Literature survey

Criteria for success:
* Supervisor has approved draft report by 20th October
* Tick-sheets filled in, approving final draft in all main categories (readability, coherent plan, grammar and style) by two proofreaders: a subject specialist and a non-specialist
* Literature survey handed in by 11th November

Figure 5.4 Example work package

information does *not* always aid clarity. The human brain can only deal with a limited number of items in one 'sitting'. The phrase, 'You cannot see the wood for the trees' speaks of too much detail actually preventing you from perceiving the higher-level structure. Use this knowledge, and some common sense, to make sure that your work packages appear readable, and coherent. Full details can appear in your own personal managerial plan, which is intended to help you get the job done and not necessarily to be shown to other people.

Finally, all the work packages can be pulled together into a larger section, sometimes known as a *work plan*. This would contain a general introduction to the work to be done, followed by the main aim, the list of objectives (top-level only), and then the work packages. Work plans nearly always go on to indicate the timing structure of the project, and that is what we will now consider in more detail.

Planning time in your project

In Chapter 2 we considered the issue of personal time management. Here we are considering project time management. It is important to note the difference. In *personal* time management, you are trying to organise *yourself*, and to manage all the activities that exist on several levels within your life. With *project* time management, you are focusing purely on completing your project, by charting the way that time will be allocated to different phases. This section will help you through this process.

Establishing all external deadlines

Before we calculate timings for the project, it is vital to note down what external deadlines already exist. Here are some questions you might want to ask:

- When is your final report due in?
- What is the last date for submitting a particular proposal?
- Are there certain periods of the year when certain activities have to take place (e.g. weather-dependent field-trips, or the availability of collaborators)?
- Do you have regular meetings with your supervisor that can be scheduled now?
- Are there specific dates when you are to do presentations?

Build up a list of all the fixed timings for the lifetime of your project. Put these in your diary immediately if you have not already done so. These are the major events that you need to work towards, and you cannot afford to forget. However, really good projects are driven from *within* and do not rely on external prompting.

Working backwards from fixed deadlines

You should 'work backwards' from these fixed deadlines, to ensure that everything is ready ahead of schedule. You can do this by deciding on times that you will have completed certain things in order to guarantee that the final deadline is met.

As an example, if your final report is due in four months time, you can work out a specific schedule guaranteed to get it completed on time or ahead of time. There is probably something you can do about the report right now (see Chapter 8 for some ideas). Make a list of all the sections of the report that need to be written. Try allocating deadlines to each section.

Working forward to allocate time

However, you should also work forward – allocating time sensibly for all the tasks in your work packages.

Inevitably, you will have to compromise. There are various ways of handling the fact that you simply do not know how long each stage of the project will take. One of these is project storyboarding, which is why we began this chapter by producing an ordered outline of tasks, without worrying too much about exactly how long each task was going to take.

In a typical project there are more tasks to do than you really have time for. So a good project plan will:

•   contain a list of all major activities in the *order* in which they need to be carried out;
•   allocate these sensibly to the time available;
•   be flexible enough to change as the project develops.

Storyboard or time-chart

In a research project, it is often the storyboard that turns out to be the most useful tool, because it helps you to concentrate on the logical *flow* of events that your project could address, rather than trying to predict accurately *how long* each section will take to complete. It is often better for a supervisor to receive a well-thought-out ordered list of tasks to be done, rather than a badly-thought-out time-based chart.

Imagine for a moment you are a supervisor and you receive Figure 5.5 from one student and Figure 5.6 from another.

Would you agree that there is something quite convincing about Plan B (Figure 5.6)? 'He's done a timetable, so it *must* be OK!' Maybe Plan A (Figure 5.5) looks a bit too undecided?

On closer inspection, however, it becomes clear that there is more substance to the planning that has gone into Plan A. It is an ordered series of tasks, which demonstrates that the student has been thinking about not only the product, but also how it is

- Literature survey (4 weeks)
- End-user questionnaire (1 week)
- Analysis of results (? 1 day ?)
- First stage design process (1–2 weeks)
- Show to end-users: more feedback (A few weeks? Not sure yet)
- Top-level software design (2 weeks?)
- Software analysis: which package? (By end of term 1)
- Coding phase 1: core algorithms (No idea; help please)
- Test phase for core algorithms (2 days maximum)
- Coding phase 2: interface device handling (Again, help)
- Test phase for interface algorithms (1 day ?)

Etc. etc.

Figure 5.5 Example student project plan (Plan A)

Week no.	1	2	3	4	5	6	7	8	9	10	11	12	13	14	15	16	17	18	19
First stage	▒	▒	▒	▒															
Supervisions		■			■	■		■		■		■			■		■		
Coding					■	■	■	■	■	■	■	■	■	■					
Testing															■	■			
Report writing																	■	■	■
Final presentation																			■

Figure 5.6 Example student project plan (Plan B)

perceived by the end user. It has an honest list of durations, with question marks to show what is not yet decided, and a direct call for help to the supervisor (who might be able to offer some guidance as to how long these things tend to take). In summary, this is a good start for a project plan, which looks as though it would be a good basis for a detailed discussion.

Plan B, by contrast, is accurate to the week number, and each phase seamlessly passes on to the next. Real-life tends to be neither time-accurate nor smooth. The student has also made the classic mistake of writing the report at the end of the project (see Chapter 8). There is also little indication that much thought has gone into *what* the project will actually do. Yet Plan B is the sort of plan most often submitted. It is a triumph of form over function. 'We need a time-chart, so here is a time-chart', yet it will be of little use in the project.

However, there are many situations when you *have* identified all the phases and they simply *must* be done within a particular time-slot. This is where a time-chart is useful, as it forces you to think about the relative proportion of time that each section of work should take. Remember, though, that if it turns out that things take longer, you will have a decision to make; do you reduce the number of phases you plan to complete? Or do you still aim to get all the planned phases complete but cut down on your expectations, doing less within each phase, or doing it to a lower quality?

Creating a time-chart

Many software packages exist to help you manage your project, and these include a wealth of sophisticated features including time-charting. However, they cannot actually do the project *thinking* for you. There is no substitute for sorting out your aims and objectives, finding out what has already been done, placing the work into a logical order, and carrying this out effectively by managing your own time.

The most common form of time-chart is the GANTT chart (this stands for Generalised Activity Normalisation TimeTable, but I'm not sure if that helps at all!). A GANTT chart is a table of information that uses word descriptions of tasks (arranged vertically in time order), and graphical representations of the time each task is meant to occupy (on a horizontal scale). The ideal GANTT chart takes up a single sheet of paper, and shows the entire project time-line in a single view. However, for bigger projects they can be made extremely complex.

The act of constructing a GANTT chart forces you to ask certain questions about every major task:

- Roughly when in the project time should this task occur?
- Are there other tasks that need to be done *before* this can even be started?
- Does the completion of this task naturally lead on to other tasks?
- How long should it take to complete?

If you have put a good deal of thought into a project storyboard, you will probably have a good idea about the answers to the first three of these questions. The last is always the hardest to answer, and is the precise reason why any form of time-charting is only ever going to be a good guess. However, it is a very useful tool for your Manager to consider on a regular basis because you can always use it to compare what is *actually* going on with what you *thought* should have been going on.

Figure 5.7 shows a typical GANTT chart, produced using Microsoft Project software, following through the ideas presented in Plan A (Figure 5.5).

Notice the following features:

- the tasks are listed in a column, working downwards in time order;
- the horizontal blocks represent the time allocated for each task;
- relationships have been added, where one task 'feeds into' the next;
- some tasks take place independently of the others.

It would be possible to expand on this GANTT chart by adding the following features:

- deadlines (e.g. initial report, final report, presentations);
- milestones (things you really want to have happened by a certain time);
- work packages (if you have developed these, you can have tasks grouped together, but linked to an appropriate work package).

Being realistic about what time you have

When you write '3 weeks' on your chart, make sure that you know what that really means for you in terms of working hours. Is this a full-time project where you are sure you will be working 40-hour weeks? Even if it is, how many of those 40 hours are really productive? On the other hand, maybe you have other commitments in your studies or your home life, which mean that each week has only 10 hours in which to work. Being honest about the number of hours you really have available will help you in your estimation of how long things should take. It helps, of course, if you have done this sort of task before, because you can judge from your previous experience how long the new task should take. Otherwise, you might want to ask other people for advice.

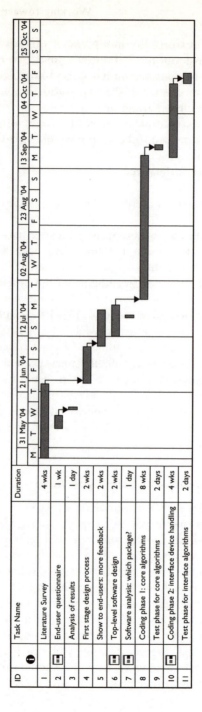

Figure 5.7 GANTT chart taken from Plan A

Alternatively, you can take the approach of simply setting the time, and *doing what you can* within that time. This is particularly useful for more open-ended tasks such as 'testing' or 'editing', where you might never finish to a perfect standard. In these situations why not set a time-limit, then stop work when the time runs out? Your approach to setting time is something about which both your Manager and Worker need to be clear. Ask for outside help if you are unsure, but make sure you have first had a go yourself before asking someone else for advice.

Summary

You should now have a storyboard (or at least a list) of key events in your project, in the order in which they need to occur. You may have worked these into a work plan that includes packages of related tasks, or you may be content with a single task list. At each stage you should know what would make a successful outcome. You should also have some idea of how you are going to spend your time on the project, and what is to be produced at each stage. You may have this all summarised on a time-chart, which your Manager can use to monitor the project as it progresses.

In the following chapter we will consider in more detail some of the best ways to communicate your ideas to other people.

Chapter 6

Communicating with others

Introduction

Everything we have discussed so far in this book relates to the *internal* dialogue that takes place between your inner Manager and Worker. This chapter concerns the *external* communications that will occur during the project, as you interact with other people. The supervision process is integral to any major project, and so we focus on the things that you can do to maximise the benefits of the important relationship between you and your supervisor. We also discuss a range of insights into the communication process in general, to ensure that you are aware of how others might view what you write and say. This leads to some specific hints about how to structure your phone calls, emails and presentations.

Other people have different priorities

In this book we have been considering how to manage yourself, create lists of tasks, and then carry out those tasks successfully. The first thing to acknowledge about contacting *other* people is that they have their *own* lists of goals and priorities that need balancing. When one person decides to contact another, there is now yet another item for that person to deal with. If someone takes the time to listen to you or help you, it is good to appreciate that they have done this at the expense of doing something else that they had previously planned to do. In later sections, we examine this in more detail, in order to learn how to minimise the disruption, and to maximise the reward for you.

For now, let us concentrate on the core communication which takes place between student and supervisor.

The supervision process

For small-scale projects and assignments there may not be a supervisor, and you are entirely responsible for managing, making decisions and completing the assignment. This section assumes that you are dealing with a major project with an assigned supervisor who indeed might have set the project in the first place. The interaction between you and your supervisor is the primary communication path in your project, so it is important that we look at ways to maximise the benefits of this relationship.

Role of the supervision process

The supervision process is the meeting of two minds. Your supervisor will usually have more experience in the general topic area, and you will have more time available to work on a sub-set of the topic area. Therefore at the end of the project, it is *you* who will be the expert in the sub-topic you have studied. Understanding this is the key to a successful relationship.

The supervisor can guide you at all stages of the process, but remember that, in a good research project, you are both working on something new, so there are no ready-packaged 'right answers'. Supervisors are often likely to answer your questions with another question, and for good reason. Consider the following two conversations.

1

Student:	I'm really stuck on this tricky problem. I need to make a decision, but should it be 'path A' or 'path B'?
Supervisor:	Path A.
Student:	OK, thanks.

2

Student:	I'm really stuck on this tricky problem. I need to make a decision, but should it be 'path A' or 'path B'?
Supervisor:	Mmm – that *is* a tricky problem! What do *you* think is the solution?
Student:	Er, [*pause*] well, path A might be the easiest to get going with, but B is the most elegant solution. However it will be expensive and will take me ages.
Supervisor:	OK, so what do you think we should do then?

Student:	Well, I suppose we could try path A, because I can at least get on with it. Then we could meet again to discuss how it went, and if it was no good, then we would have to re-think about path B.
Supervisor:	Seems like a good idea. Are you happy to get on with that?
Student:	OK, thanks.

Notice that in both conversations the opening and closing sentences are the same. But do you notice how the learning process is very different? The irony is that many students *want* the first conversation. They want to 'learn from the guru', and 'be told the right way to go'. Look again at the first conversation. The student is left with the feeling that the supervisor already knows the answer. The student probably has no idea of why path A has been chosen, so really not much has been learnt. Worse still, in the final examination someone might ask, 'Why did you take path A?', and the honest (but not very impressive) reply is, 'Because my supervisor told me to'. In other words, it reinforces the student's view that they do not know the answer, and that other people are somehow better than them at being able to find an answer.

In contrast, in the second conversation, *because* the supervisor holds back from giving a straight answer, several things have occurred:

- the supervisor understands that there is no easy choice;
- the student feels that they have an important say in the process;
- the student has been allowed to come up with their own reasons for the choice;
- the student will be able to justify this decision to anyone else in the future.

The supervisor is also your main link with your educational establishment. So, he or she needs to know as soon as possible if anything goes wrong (illness, lack of focus, change of topic, or any other circumstance that affects your work). The supervisor will also help you to be aware of the arrangements and deadlines that concern your project, but remember that it is *you* who needs to manage the details of your workload so that those deadlines are met.

In summary, your supervisor:

- is the link between you and your educational institution;
- usually has more experience in running projects;
- usually knows more about the topic area, at least to begin with;
- is there for you to discuss things with, *not* to 'tell you the answers';
- can help you to continually review your progress;
- needs to know about any problems sooner rather than later;
- does not have a big block of time to work on detailed projects;
- needs you as part of the team to push forward the research field;
- will *not* be the expert in your sub-topic by the end of the project;
- has all sorts of other commitments to deal with that you should be aware of.

Understanding the supervisor's priorities

Whenever you are communicating with other people, you should (wherever possible) be aware of some of their concerns, demands and priorities. Whilst it is true that your supervisor has the very important role of helping you in your project, they also have hundreds of other tasks to do. A university supervisor, for example, has all their *other* students to supervise (at both undergraduate, masters and doctoral level), each with different topics and schedules to manage. You might be surprised to find out that *all* of these supervision commitments constitute just a small part of the job. You might refer to him or her as 'my supervisor' but the job role of 'lecturer', for example, extends way beyond looking after project students. There are the regular lecturing commitments (and preparing a lecture takes a *lot* longer than the hour or so it takes to deliver it). Then there is the research role, by which many academics and universities are assessed. Research applications take months to prepare and a high proportion face rejection; but credit is only given for acceptances. When grants are awarded, then the work is committed to be carried out; large-scale, risky, experimental projects and teams of people need to be managed. Then there are the administrative tasks: Boards of Studies to manage the curriculum, exam marking and feedback, exam meetings, disciplinary procedures, letters of reference to write for past students, staff–student liaison meetings, and minutes to prepare, new courses to develop, interviews for prospective students and researchers, journal papers to be written, books to write, conferences to referee, conferences to attend, plan and present ongoing work at . . . and the list goes on and on.

This is not intended to make you feel sorry for your 'poor old supervisor', but it is intended to help you to understand the commitments and perspective of the 'other half' of your supervision process.

As a specific example, imagine that you would benefit from some feedback on something you have written (perhaps 20 pages of a project report). Because you have decided that you want this it would be easy to think of your supervisor as some sort of feedback service, and ask them to 'look at this before our meeting tomorrow'. However, now that you are aware of some of the commitments that your supervisor is already dealing with as a matter of course, you might find other ways of approaching the issue, such as:

> 'I would really like some feedback on Chapter 1 of my report. Ideally I need this by the end of the month to allow me to respond to any feedback while writing my next chapters which I hope to do next month. Do you have any time in the next two weeks to look at this?'

Note that in order to allow this much time (i.e. waiting two weeks for feedback) you will have had to identify the need early. In other words *it is important to plan ahead, if you wish to effectively (and courteously) use someone else's resources.*

Knowledge of your supervisor's other commitments will also help when you are structuring your regular contact with them, as we will see in the next section.

Maximising the benefits of the supervision process

There are no fixed rules about supervisions. You will arrange with your supervisor how often you should meet, whether to pre-book those meetings in advance, or whether to 'wait until one is needed'. However, in the next three paragraphs we will look at three issues that will transform the supervision process:

- prepare for meetings
- co-operate in research
- move from dependence to independence.

Prepare for meetings by ensuring that you know what you want to get out of each particular meeting and letting your supervisor know this. You may want to try producing an *agenda* (a structured plan of issues to be discussed) which can be sent to the supervisor in advance of the meeting. This helps you both to be clear about what you want to achieve. Your supervisor can add extra items to that agenda, and this results in a joint list of what needs discussing. This is not to imply that your meetings need to be terribly formal, but rather that you both take part in the meeting knowing what you want as outcomes. This also helps your supervisor to 'tune-in' to your specific research topic and problems, given that for hours beforehand they will be working on many of the other commitments outlined above.

Co-operate in research by showing an interest in the *other* things that the supervisor is involved with. People generally enjoy discussing their work with other people, so why not ask your supervisor about his or her other research project? By this process you will gain a wider view of your project and where it fits into an area of research. Also, subtly, this sort of discussion makes you both feel more like a *team*, rather than a hierarchy.

Move from dependence to independence by using the supervision process to learn to be a researcher in your own right. At the start of a project you may need a lot of guidance in the topic, and in the processes of study. Supervisions may be packed with questions from you and guidance from the supervisor. During the middle stage of the project supervisions become discussions, and towards the end – *you* are the expert in your area, demonstrating to the supervisor what you have done or discovered. A supervisor who 'makes himself redundant' by working with a student until they are a confident, independent worker, has probably done a good job. But this can only work if you play your part, and gradually take on more responsibility for the management of your own project. See again the section in Chapter 1 on 'the dependent worker'.

Structuring your communications

Other people's mind-sets

There is a time in most children's development when it suddenly dawns on them that not everyone sees the world through their eyes. Even in adulthood we often only see a particular situation from our own perspective. But actually everyone else is seeing a different view and thinking unique thoughts. Every person's brain has built up its own way of viewing, listening to and interpreting the world. Two people may look at the same space yet see completely different things. This may seem a very philosophical discussion to be having at this point, but it is at the very heart of the art of communication. Successful communication *bridges the gap* between one person's view of the world and another's.

Revealing information logically

Imagine that someone said to you:

> 'The banana is brighter in colour, and therefore it should score higher than the fish. However the burger is hidden within its packaging, so you have only your knowledge of the advertising to tell you what is actually inside. The can doesn't feature as I have implied that you are hungry.'

Would you have any idea what the person was talking about? It sounds rather like the ramblings of someone whose mind is altered by various chemicals. Imagine now that you heard the following preamble, leading up to the same words:

> 'This is the third session in our series of lectures* looking at the health issues surrounding food in the western world. Today we're looking at the effect of food packaging and advertising on the choices that people make when confronted with several, visually different, alternative foods. Let's start with a rather artificial exercise. On the desk in front of me I have laid out some examples of different food types which clearly look distinctive. We have a banana, a can of fish, a burger in a cardboard container, and a can of fizzy drink. Imagine that you come into the room and are hungry. I'm going to ask you to choose one item, but you only have 2 seconds to do this. Choose now, 1, 2, STOP. Hands up if you chose the burger? The banana? The

* Apologies to anyone who studies this sort of stuff for real – this is an entirely fictitious argument invented to make the point. Any similarity to a real lecture is entirely coincidental.

fish? Interesting – most of you went for the burger. Do you know that if you were *reading* this most of you would go for the banana? Somehow your visual system is influencing the choice. So, how did your visual system and brain handle this? Well, suppose your eyes and brain produce a "points" system to rank the items. The banana is brighter in colour, and therefore it should score higher than the fish. The burger is hidden within its packaging, so you have only your knowledge of the advertising to tell you what is actually inside. The can doesn't feature as I have implied that you are hungry not thirsty. . . .'

Whatever you think of the fictitious lecture, did you find that the second extract flowed better? Then the same text (which was rather bizarre when seen out of context) made reasonable sense when your brain had been given the correct 'cues'.

If we analyse what your brain was saying when it read the first paragraph, it would probably sound something like this:

Paragraph: The banana . . .
Your brain: *What* banana? Who *are* you and *what* are you talk-
               ing about?
Paragraph: . . . is brighter in colour . . .
Your brain: Brighter than *what*? I still don't know *which* banana
               you are talking about, and now you're comparing it
               with some *other* object I don't even *know* about.
               And I *still* don't know why I'm listening to you
               anyway.
Paragraph: . . . and therefore it should score higher than the fish.
Your brain: Now come on – you're just having a laugh! Even
               if I knew *which* banana you meant, are you now
               saying that because it is *brighter* than some other, as
               yet undescribed object, it scores more *points* (in some,
               as yet undescribed competition) than a *fish* which
               has just popped out of your mind? And who *are* you
               anyway? This is too hard. All this talk of food is
               making me hungry. Now, what shall I have for tea?
               Now I should have some fruit but I've got that half-
               eaten burger from yesterday . . .

And thus another student switches off in a lecture before the first sentence is complete!

Actually, keeping people awake when teaching is another issue altogether. But at least a lecturer following the second paragraph would have a chance of engaging with the audience. Let us consider how this was achieved:

- it reminded the listeners of where they were (third in a lecture series);
- it stated the overall topic (health issues relating to western food);
- it stated the purpose of this particular communication (choices and adverts);
- it then used a visual example (bananas, etc. on a table);
- it used audience interaction (making a real choice).

Etc., etc.

In other words, because everyone comes to a lecture with a different mind-set, it makes sense to reveal the context in a logical order. This gives every listener's brain a chance to catch up with and process what the lecturer is trying to say.

Peter Thompson (2000) describes how the brain is like a computer filing system, which needs prompting to open each file. A good piece of communication will provide prompts for the listener to 'open the appropriate file' in their heads.

For example, if you have been struggling with a piece of computer code, and you decide to see the lecturer or teacher concerned, it would be best not to say:

Student: [*Knocks on lecturer's door*]
Lecturer: [*Sighing, as the grant application is put aside yet again*] Come in!
Student: Hi – I've got a problem with this bit of code [*pointing to it*]. It won't do what I want. What's wrong with it?
Lecturer: Remind me; which course are you on . . . ?

This understandable 'diving in' on the part of the student happens often, and occurs because the student's brain is highly focused on the problem. The lecturer, in contrast, is still thinking about his own work, and (as you can tell from the above dialogue) is not even sure who this student is.

Your starting-point is not theirs

In the previous section, we saw how people can be confused if you just 'dive in'. This applies to students talking to lecturers, just as much as it applies to lecturers delivering material to students. But it is also true for everyday conversations. Have you ever stopped someone in mid-conversational flow and said, 'I'm sorry, but I have *no* idea what you are talking about'?

This is actually a very common problem for those who appear in front of others: lecturers, celebrities, musicians, etc. The audience feel that they know the person so well that they assume that this recognition is reciprocated, whereas this is clearly impossible. I met one celebrity who has fine-tuned some amazing memory feats so that when he encounters people for a second time he can say things like, 'Hello Jill, how are the twins doing?', and Jill smiles to herself that she is clearly valued by this celebrity. His experience before learning these memory techniques was to honestly say, 'Hello? Do I know you?' and then watch the crestfallen look as the person realised that this celebrity who had been in their living room (on the telly) had no idea who they were.

People typically do not think about the point of view of the person they are talking to. Therefore, when you start talking to someone, help their brain to catch up with yours, by setting the context.

Let us return to our student with the coding problem. Maybe this next encounter would be more productive?

Student:	[*Knocks on lecturer's door*]
Lecturer:	[*Sighing, as the grant application is put aside yet again*] Come in.
Student:	Hi – my name's Michael, and I emailed you earlier?
Lecturer:	Ah yes, I remember. I asked you to call round.
Student:	Yes, thanks. I'm on the second year computing course unit, and we've got the flight control assignment to do. It's due in at the end of the week but I've got stuck with one section and don't know how to move forward.
Lecturer:	OK, do you have a print-out of your code with you?
Student:	Yes, here it is. OK, so there are three main sections: [*pointing to the code*] the stored data, the incoming

flight data, and the processing algorithm. My problem is in the processing stage. It's around here [*pointing to the general area*]. This particular section should combine the stored data with the incoming data, but I don't think it is working.

Lecturer: Which bit in particular do you think is not working? . . .

Etc.

In this example, the student implicitly acknowledges that the lecturer has been concentrating on something else, by reminding him of the context ('my name's Michael, and I emailed you earlier?'). The rising pitch indicated by the question mark is subtle, but important. It is a polite way of saying 'remember'? And of course as soon as the lecturer remembers, half the battle is won. The grant application is temporarily forgotten and the lecturer now needs to know what the context is. The student has reminded him that his name is Michael, but now sets the context brilliantly by declaring which course he is on and which assignment the problem concerns. This 'opens' these topics in the lecturer's mind, and Michael now explains his situation ('due in at the end of the week but I've got stuck with one section'). The process continues, and the encounter is focused and creative.

How could you plan to improve your next communication so that the listener/reader is more prepared and therefore follows what you are saying?

Different forms of communication

Having considered how to reveal information to the person you are communicating with, we now take a brief look at the ways in which you might actually perform the act of communication. In the next sections we compare the use of email with phone calls and visits (both unplanned and pre-arranged).

Email

Most people in a college or university use email extensively. Members of staff will use it every day as part of their jobs, and so will be monitoring it fairly carefully (although you will discover that different people have varying rates of response when sent a message!). The best thing about email is that you do not actually disturb anyone's thought process by sending it.* People tend to read their email when they are ready to do so, or when they just need a break. The main point is that they are actively *expecting* new messages and new information. This is a good state for your recipient to be in when you wish to initiate a communication. The entire process may be suitable to be carried out by email (e.g. a request for information, a summary report, or a question about an assignment, etc.). However, you can also use an email to arrange to have a phone conversation if needed, or to meet in person.

Therefore, if in doubt – *start the communication process with an email*.

If you get no reply, do not be afraid to send a copy a few days later. Sometimes emails get accidentally deleted, or removed by filters, so politely point out that you sent an email a while ago and that you have taken the liberty of sending it again. You might want to check that you are providing sensible message 'subjects'. Consider the following emails arriving in your inbox:

From	Subject	Size
Druggy005@aol.com	Cheap drugs BUY IT NOW	15KB
DittyBoy	help me	943KB
Henry James		3KB
Michael Connor	2nd Year Flight Control assignment enquiry	7KB
Helen T. Robbetts	Sell your endowment policies today	16KB

If you were a lecturer (receiving over 100 messages per day) which ones would you delete without opening? Most people would *only* open Michael Connor's message because it had a clearly relevant subject line. Poor Henry James is a first year student (whom the lecturer is not familiar with yet) who has put no subject message in his desperate email about exam problems, so it is promptly deleted as if it were SPAM. And what about Jim Fisher, the 3rd year who needs to talk to you about his financial problems? You never received his email? Or does he unfortunately use

---

* Actually, if they *are* disturbed by your incoming message going 'ding' and they stop work to answer it, this is at least their *choice*. I turn off all email sounds, and respond to incoming messages only when I am ready. This means that emails do not interrupt me, and they are therefore less disturbing.

the 'fun' alias-name DittyBoy, and the emotional but completely unhelpful 'help me' in the subject line, which makes it look like a typical SPAM appeal?

We will return to the content of the email in the next major section, 'Asking people for help'.

Telephone

For some communication tasks telephoning is a much better way of getting in touch. People in certain types of job (such as receptionists, secretaries, personal assistants, journalists, etc.) treat incoming phone calls with top priority. You also have the satisfaction of having spoken to 'a real person' and thus have some feeling of how successful the communication has been.

However, there are many downsides, including the following (fictitious) responses:

- 'I'm sorry but he is on the phone at the moment, would you like to waste an unknown amount of your time listening to some music while you wait?'
- 'Welcome to the automated menu service. I will now automatically occupy an unspecified amount of your time, and give you a list of services which do not cover the reason for your call. If this is OK, please press 1 now . . .'
- 'Er – hello – I'm in a meeting right now. Can I call you back? Better still, call my secretary and he will take a message'

In other words you cannot guarantee that the person will be available to talk, and you need to be prepared to wait, leave messages, call back later, or use another form of communication. You are also disturbing that person's current work-flow, and as we have seen it is advisable to minimise this disruption where possible. This is the reason for the suggestion to email first where possible (which also gives you a written record of the communication), then arrange to speak on the phone at a given time if you need to discuss things more interactively.

'Dropping in'

Please think twice (or more) before making a random call to someone's office door. You will either find them:

- not there
- busy in a meeting (which you have just interrupted)
- on the telephone (which is awkward to leave to answer the door)
- working on something else.

In other words you are almost *guaranteed* to be interrupting the person you want help from, and almost certain to find them in a mental state *not* conducive to answering your problem. When you are on the receiving end of such a visit it is rather frustrating when the visitor looks around the room and (if full of people) says, 'Sorry – I see you're busy', or if empty says, 'Hi – are you busy?' or 'Is this a good time to see you?' The true answers to these questions are, 'Yes, I *am* busy' or 'No, by definition, this is *not* a good time to visit'.*

Use email instead to *arrange* a visit, which you are both then expecting, and which, as a consequence, will be much more constructive.

Asking people for help

Even though your supervisor will be your main contact for help throughout your project, there will be times when you need to ask others for help. This might be, for example, asking another academic for some information on their research, or asking a company if they can give you some technical guidance on their product. In this section we consider some of the good (and bad) ways to ask people for help.

How not to do it

Imagine for a moment that you are an academic in a university. You are just wondering how to proceed with the day's jobs when the following email arrives. Read it and note your reaction.

---

* The exception to this rule is if the person is known to operate an 'open-door' policy, where dropping in is actively encouraged. In such a situation there is still no disadvantage with making the first contact by email, saying 'Is it OK for me to drop round now, to talk about. . . .'

Dear Professr,
You are an expert in computers. My supervisor is ill at the moment, and I need some recommendations of how I can do my project which is in your area. Please cud u send me the most important references in this area, and tell me the most imprtant things I shud be doing. Please get back to me promptyl as I have only a few weeks left on my projectg.
Yours,
[student at another university!]

How does it make you feel? Does it make you want to help the person? Maybe you reacted with some of the following thoughts:

1   The whole thing is shoddily put together as if the sender does not really care about this communication at all.
2   This is a student from *another* university, with which you have no contact or commitment to in any way at all.
3   Why should you do somebody else's work for them?
4   Surely the student should urgently contact people in his own department to get something done about their supervision process?
5   The student is asking you to spend time (that you are desperately short of) in reading his mail, putting together a list of references (which is not well defined at all), and giving project guidance about a completely undefined project!
6   He has the cheek to request a prompt reply, without any reference to the fact that you might have something else to do, and has nothing to do with them anyway!
Etc., etc.

As you see, just a few hurried words, written from one's own perspective, can create a very bad reaction in the reader. You, the reader, felt imposed upon, and the student ended up with nothing as the academic deleted his email.

Yet this is the sort of message it is easy to write if you are fully immersed in your project and simply think of other people as 'ready sources of information'.

Decide when communication is necessary

A golden rule of communication is to do it sparingly, and after much thought.

Maybe some of you have been plagued by SPAM emails or junk post. The people sending this stuff do not care about you or your email in-basket, or whether you are offended by its contents. They just fire their message to as many people as possible in the hope that one or two will answer and buy their product. Therefore, an uninvited message that has little relevance to you, and is sent out to many people, is SPAM. The above message from the student was practically SPAM. If you are going to communicate with someone, you need to make sure it is not perceived as such. In the following section there are some hints about how to do this.

Ensuring your communication creates a good reaction

- Make it *personal* (i.e. a single message written and sent to one person).
- Explain why you are contacting *them* (and not somebody else).
- Make it *interesting* for them (the person reading it is a person with their own priorities. Why should they spend any time on this at all?).
- Be as *specific* as possible. Ask a simple question which you think they are the right person to answer.
- Be aware that the recipient will have little time available, so make sure that what you are asking them could be done quickly, if not immediately, and that you do not appear to be demanding it.
- Consider what you are *offering* the person. Re-read the above email, and consider how *you* would react to it. There is nothing to be gained by replying. A good communication should acknowledge that the recipient needs to get something from this.

All of this takes time and effort. And this, once again, is the heart of it. Rushed, sloppily worded communications are not usually effective, yet the email and text culture has made speedy messages possible. Carefully worded, interesting communications that offer something to the recipient are more likely to get a positive reply.

Imagine that the same student had sent the following letter. This example includes one of my own research fields as an example of how such a letter needs to be customised and relevant to the person you are writing to.

Dear Dr Hunt,

I am a student from [*another university*] working on new electronic musical instruments. I have been reading about your work on sonification, but I am unsure how the two fields relate. I know this is a busy exam time, but I wonder if you would be able to help me with a short answer to a particular problem in your field?

In your paper for the Multimedia Data Workshop you described an ideal interactive sonification system as requiring 'control intimacy similar to an acoustic musical instrument'. Would you be willing to explain this comment further, as I would like to refer to it in my thesis? Alternatively do you know of any other information sources which deal with this problem? I would be very happy to send you the completed thesis at the end of the project if you are interested.

Many thanks in anticipation,

[*Student's name*]

This is a completely different entity, and if I received it, I would probably give it a positive reply, maybe almost immediately. The person has clearly been reading my work, and has a question to answer, which explains their motivation in contacting me. They are interested in what I have to say, yet acknowledge that I probably will be busy. They offer something in return (a copy of their thesis in an area of interest to me) as an extra incentive to reply (although this is not always necessary). To summarise: address your communication in a non-assuming way, explain clearly why you are contacting a particular person and ask specific questions that can probably be answered.

Presenting your ideas to others

At some point in your project you may be required to do a stand-up presentation to explain your work. This may take the form of a research seminar where an unknown number of interested people come along to hear about your project. Or it might be a formal part of the assessment where everyone doing a research project is expected to present the outcomes (or the progress) of their work. You might also be asked to present your work at a conference (see Chapter 10 for more on this).

Whatever the setting, it is natural to worry about public speaking, but in this section we present a few practical techniques that will help you to prepare better for the talk, and – who knows – maybe even *enjoy* the process!

Establishing the audience

By far the most important thing you can do is to work out *who* you are talking to and to determine their *reason* for being there. It matters enormously whether people have *chosen* to come to your talk. If so, it means that they are already an interested audience. On the other hand if people *have* to be there (for example as a requirement for a course or assessment) then you will need to work harder to interest them in what you are saying.

A really good hint is to work out 'what they know already'. As an illustration, imagine that the audience consists primarily of your fellow students. In this case you can assume your common knowledge of the entire course so far, but you *cannot* assume knowledge of your particular project area. Your job in this case is to take the audience from the knowledge you had *before* you started your project (which should be similar to their current mind-set) up to the point you are at now.

It is also useful to gauge (in advance if possible) the predicted numbers of people in the audience. This will affect how you choose to deliver your talk. For a small number of people you can be chatty and informal, but a larger audience will require more energy from you, and more of a performance.

Methods of presentation

Your next choice should be to choose which method you will use to deliver the talk, as this will determine the way you gather materials for the presentation. Here we consider some of the options available to you, and consider the pros and cons of each.

Talking without notes

This is quite a scary way of proceeding, but may be highly appropriate for a small audience (or any other environment that is more forgiving). You need to be confident about what you are saying, and have either memorised your talk, or be willing to improvise it. The advantages of this method are that you are looking at your audience the whole time, and are more likely to interact with them. It is also easy to use a blackboard or whiteboard to illustrate your talk as you go. If you do this well, it can make for a compelling and confident talk, but it takes *lots* of practice.

Talking with notes

This is a 'safer' (and more common way) to proceed with a talk. This allows you to think through the structure of the talk in advance, and to give yourself cues (for example 'play sound example no. 1 from the CD') at certain points.

The detail that you put on the notes will determine the style of the delivery. At one extreme you could have a *pre-prepared speech*. Here, everything is written down in full, and you simply read out your own words. Whilst this reduces the potential error (because all your words have been formed in advance) it also drastically reduces the potential for change and opportunities for eye-contact with the audience, which would help you to respond to their reactions. Also, unless you are well-practised at speech-giving, it can sound very stilted. A final problem is that the words we *write* are usually different to those we *speak*. Phrases that work formally on paper can sound very 'stiff' when delivered to an audience.

So instead you could use *'bullet-pointed notes'*, such as:

- welcome
- why I am talking about TV advertising
- VIDEO example.

Etc.

These are intended to act as reminders to you. You will need to turn these into sentences *as you are delivering them*. If this sounds daunting, just remember that this is what you do every time you have a conversation with someone. So, the above bullet-points might become:

> 'Welcome to the afternoon session. I hope lunch wasn't so big that you all fall asleep! Today I'll be talking about the effect of TV advertising on the dietary habits of the general population. Let's start by taking a look at the following video example . . .'

The advantage is that you can change the style and mood of your delivery according to the specific audience. This is something that gets easier with practice.

Some people have their notes on A4 paper on a lectern, whereas some write them on postcards. The lectern is more formal, whereas the postcards allow you to move around more easily.

Talking using a slideshow

This is a very common way of delivering a presentation nowadays. Your talk is marked out by a series of slides (containing text and graphics), which are displayed to the audience. This is typically done by using either *pre-printed acetates* or *computer presentation software*. The audience can also be a given a printout of the slides, often many slides to one page, with space to take notes.

Pre-printed slides (which can be handwritten using acetate pens, or can be printed out from a computer) allow you to physically manipulate the current slide. If this is done well, it can be a highly effective way of working. Some advantages are that you can re-order your slides (or miss some out if running short of time), and that you can reveal sections of the slide to your audience by placing a sheet of paper on the projector. You will be able to see what is coming up next, but the audience cannot. This helps your flow. However, some disadvantages are that if the slides are dropped, the talk becomes hopelessly out of order, and if handled wrongly you can point with a shaking hand to a slide which is slanting on the screen and this is very disconcerting for the audience.

It is now common practice to project slides 'live' from a computer. There are none of the problems of lining up the slide, and indeed there are the advantages of being able to trigger sound and video material from within the presentation. However, many presentations are done with a standard (usually the default) layout and text font, and dramatically different talks can ironically end up 'all looking the same'. It is also harder for the presenter to see what is coming up next, which makes it vital for you to have a set of notes, showing the slide order, and any extra comments you wish to make.

Here are some guidelines that will help you with the layout of the slides if you are preparing your first presentation:

• Keep the text on each slide short. The audience will then listen to what *you* have to say, rather than just reading the slide.

- If you want your slides to contain lots of detail, make a 'full details' version for yourself, print this out as your 'notes', then make an abbreviated version for the audience to see.
- Try not to read out the text that is on the slide (unless you specifically want the audience to remember a particular statement by rote). This does not help the audience as everyone is reading at different speeds.
- Supplement the text with graphics. It can make your presentation look more individual, as pure-text slides tend to get boring. Also lots of people in your audience will respond better to graphical ideas (such as cartoons, photographs, block diagrams, etc.) than to text.
- Be careful with the use of animated effects (such as each bullet-point whizzing in from the left, accompanied by a 'wheeeeeeee' sound). This causes great amusement when you are setting it up, and you may get one laugh in the presentation. But after that it becomes annoying to everyone.

Planning the presentation

The planning phase is vital. It is here that you consider what the audience currently knows, and what you want them to know by the end of your presentation. Do not start making slides or notes until you know *why* you are giving the talk, and *who* will be listening.

The order in which you reveal information to the audience affects how it is received. A lot can be learned by watching TV documentaries, and studying the ways in which they attract and keep a very varied audience. A typical documentary will begin with something to catch your attention – maybe even before the main titles! Then it will give you some background to the story. Note carefully the mix of styles: a formal, plainly spoken narrator tells you the 'facts', which are often supplemented by interviews with the people involved, telling their stories in enthusiastic first-person language, often supported by pictures, photos, dramatic reconstructions or computer-generated images.

You may find it helpful to draw up a mind-map (see Chapter 3) of ideas for your own presentation, which you can then annotate in numerical order. This allows a good compromise between free-thinking (mind-mapping) and ordering information into a sensible flow (numbering).

Finally, you must rehearse the talk. This is especially important if (as is often the case) you are speaking to a time-limit. You can rehearse it 'in your head', but it is much better to speak it through out loud, and even better with a friendly audience (made up of your family, friends or focus group).

Giving the talk

On the day of your presentation it is strongly advisable to get to the room as early as possible. This will allow you to ensure that your slides can be shown properly. This is particularly important if you are hoping to connect up your own laptop to some existing audiovisual equipment. It also gives you time to 'get the feel' of the room – working out where you are going to stand, and what it feels like standing in the position you will be doing your presentation.

If someone is 'chairing' your session it is good to meet with them and to make sure that they have enough information about you to be able to introduce you appropriately to the audience. You should double-check how much time you have been allocated. Ideally, agree a signal with the session chair to inform you, say, when you have five minutes left. Work out in your own mind how you will react when you receive this signal, depending on where you are in your presentation.

Another advantage of arriving at your presentation room early is that your setting up is done privately, instead of frantically in front of a waiting audience. You also get to see the audience arriving one by one. This can help to calm the nerves by seeing your audience as individuals who have come along to your talk.

As you are being introduced, take some deep breaths, then begin your presentation with a confident smile and a welcome (no matter how you are feeling). Most presenters learn to appreciate the nerves beforehand, knowing that it gives them the edge of concentration that they need for their talk.

It seems to be a natural law of presentations that they take longer than when you rehearsed them! So be prepared how to handle running over time. If you receive a signal that you are nearing the end of your time, then by far the best thing to do is to calmly say, 'Thank you. OK, I'm running a bit over time, so I'll move straight to the conclusions', then do exactly that and finish on time. No audience will thank you for rushing through all your slides at high speed and still finishing late. Once a time warning has been given – accept it, and gracefully bring your talk to a conclusion.

If you get a chance, encourage some people you trust to give you some feedback on the talk. Did they understand what you were saying? Was it too fast or too slow? Were the slides readable? Do they have any other suggestions for improvement? Write down their suggestions and refer to them next time you plan a talk.

Summary

This chapter has looked at how to communicate your work with others. The supervision role is a special relationship within any major project, and during supervisions you can try out many of these ideas. Be careful *how* and *when* you approach other people for help. Be aware that they carry with them a huge list of unseen problems and priorities, and you need to ensure that your communication is received well. Choose the appropriate medium, starting where possible with email, and following up with other media. Understand that people's brains do not start out containing what you wish to communicate to them; the essence of communication is to find a way to get your message across. This is true whether you are in a supervision meeting, writing an email to a person who does not know you, or presenting your work in front of a group of other people.

The next chapter takes a look at some of the common things that can go wrong with large projects, and gives you strategies for overcoming these problems.

Chapter 7

Common problems

Introduction

In this chapter we examine some of the common problems that anyone could encounter when carrying out a large-scale piece of solo work. You may come across some of these, all of these, or none of them! If you *do* run into them, then this chapter contains strategies and suggestions for overcoming each type of problem.

Getting stuck

One of the most common negative situations that people experience when running a project is 'getting stuck'. It happens to nearly everyone at some point in a major project.* You just do not seem to be making progress with part or all of the project. This is usually accompanied by feelings of fear ('I'm going to fail my degree') and inadequacy ('I'm just no good at this'). In this section we encourage you to face the fear, identify the problem, and work through a tried and tested means of 'un-sticking' the problem to get you moving again.

Why are you really stuck?

The first thing that you need to do is to face the problem. So often, we discover that being stuck is not the result of an external event, but rather an unsolved *internal* mental block. Because of this you might well be experiencing being stuck as a *mental state of failure.*

---

* You might be interested to know that this entire chapter came about as a direct result of being stuck for four weeks on another section of this book (I'll leave you to guess which one).

'It's *no* good – I'm just not making *any* progress'

'Everyone else is really getting on with *their* projects'

'I just *don't* know what to do'

'I'm just *not* engaged with this project'

Have you noticed how each of the above statements is an expression of negative emotion? Each statement says nothing about how to take action to get out of the situation. This is exactly what you need to do to get unstuck; you first need to flick a mental switch from this position:

'I'm not feeling very good about my lack of progress'

to this position:

'I have encountered a problem; now I am going to find a solution to it'

Without this switch being flicked, you would probably remain depressed and continue to blame external events, however relevant or irrelevant. As an example, imagine a student saying this:

'I'm completely stuck on my project because my supervisor is ill.'

This places the blame somewhere else and gives you an excuse not to do anything! Flick the mental switch and the same situation turns into this:

'My supervisor is ill, so I either need to identify something else in the project that I can be getting on with, or (if the illness is longer than a week or so) get in touch with the department to see if there is any other temporary support.'

This switch-flicking is a very simple concept, but it works because it reminds us that we really are in charge of our own work, not anybody else, nor any undesirable external event.

Exactly what is stuck?

Once you have acknowledged that it is *you* that are stuck, and that you are going to do something about it, then you can move on to identifying exactly what is stuck. Some of the negative feelings outlined above are allowed to thrive simply because you have not defined exactly what the problem is.

Taking the above example, if you think that the problem is that your supervisor is ill, you are wrong. That is simply a *fact* that relates to your project. What you probably mean (if you think about it for a minute or so) is more like this:

> 'My supervisor is ill. I was not expecting this, and I was rather hoping to get a decision this week about whether I should take "path A" or "path B". I feel rather unprepared to make that decision, and I wanted some advice.'

This is not only much more honest, but it throws the problem back to you:

> 'I need to make a decision on whether to do A or B, but I feel unprepared'

Because this problem is back with you, you can start to do something about it. So let us spend a little time to remove the negative feelings and start thinking of some positive action. The next section encourages you to focus on possible solutions to, or ways around, the problem.

What will 'being un-stuck' look and feel like?

To help you think positively, you need to be thinking about *solutions*, rather than wallowing in the negative feelings associated with the problem. So, ask yourself the question, 'What will being un-stuck look like or feel like?' Imagine for a moment that sometime in the immediate future the problem is solved, or you have found a way round. You may come up with several ideas, so write them down quickly, or produce a mind-map (as in Chapter 3).

Taking our situation above that you need a decision about option A or B, but your supervisor is not around to discuss it, here are a few mental pictures you might paint to visualise the problem already solved or worked around:

1   You imagine yourself working away happily on another part of the project, which you can make progress on without your supervisor's presence *(working around the problem)*.
2   You visualise yourself exploring options A and B in more depth, so that you gain confidence in making the decision. When your supervisor returns you are able to recommend one particular option *(taking charge of the problem based on your own understanding of the issues)*.
3   You see and hear yourself in a meeting with your supervisor, having a discussion about options A and B, and imagining exactly what he or she would say about each option *(creative thinking to give yourself some extra information)*.

The irony is that while picturing mental scene (3) (above) you might realise, with a smile, that your supervisor would be quite likely to say 'well, what do *you* think?' In this case the whole notion that you are 'stuck' because your supervisor is ill is false. You are stuck because there is a decision to be made, and all you needed in this case was the courage to make the decision yourself, once you have gained further information.

How can I put this into action and get un-stuck?

The final step is vital to becoming un-stuck. You need to turn the creative ideas into definite actions, which you schedule into your management system. This might mean entering a slot in your calendar where you will do the work, or it might be an action on your planner, or even an entry in your project list. If you have identified a specific action and you can do it now, then do it.

However, you may have come up with creative ideas that are not immediately actionable. You will need to break these down into action steps using the sorts of processes described in Chapters 2 and 3.

Imagine your creative breakthrough is that 'you need to know more about options A and B, and then make the decision yourself'. In this example you might identify the following tasks that need to be done:

- Do a web-search on options A and B.
- Create a mind-map with the pros and cons of each option.
- Make a decision (by Friday) concerning which option I should take.
- Write a one-page summary of the options, the decision and the reasons for choosing it. (This will be an invaluable memory aid for later discussion with your supervisor, and for putting in your report. It also acts a 'statement of closure', which declares in writing that you have taken charge of the problem, considered the options, made a decision, and have now moved on.)

Each of the above steps would need to be put into your system either as an action or a mini-project. Put deadlines on them, then get them done as soon as you can. You are now free.

The act of getting going again after being stuck can often be enough to completely turn your feelings around; from resignation to successful productivity. If you are stuck on something, therefore, try following the above steps until you have something specific that you can *do* to get you moving again. This process is summarised in the diagram shown in Figure 7.1.

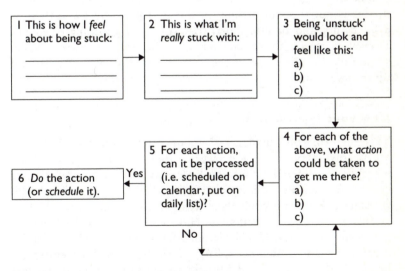

Figure 7.1 Summary of the process of becoming un-stuck

Losing focus

As you get to the core of your project, where a lot of practical work is done, it is possible to lose your focus and become *too* engrossed in your work to involve your Manager. The worst thing about this problem is that you do not notice it happening. At least you *know* when you are stuck! With loss of focus you are often busily working away, but on the wrong things.

You will eventually discover your loss of focus by noticing one of the following symptoms:

* Someone else asks you what you are doing. You reply in enthusiastic detail. They counter by asking, 'but how does that meet your main *goal*? I thought you were doing . . .'. And then it dawns on you that you are not working towards your aim and objectives.
* You develop a gnawing sense of unease that 'something isn't quite right', but you do not let yourself think about it because you are 'just too busy'. One day you realise that the unease was simply your Manager calling out to you from his internal prison cell.

It is easy to lock away the Manager when you are busy, because you have so much to do and so little time. But, if you think about it, this is not the wisest thing to do. It is precisely *when* there is a lot to do, and time is short, that you *need* good management. However urgent the circumstances, you should *always* make some time to take stock of the current situation and to create an up-to-date plan.

How your focus is lost

This loss of your managerial focus often happens when you are deeply involved in your work (analysing a piece of music, searching for references, writing a piece of computer code, etc.). In general, when you are immersed in Worker mode, you can easily get sidetracked from your plans without even noticing.

This is a natural human state. Have you ever wasted some time browsing on the World Wide Web? Maybe you started looking for a reference about Wagner's *Ring Cycle* but somehow ended up browsing the intricacies of Mongolian pig farming. How did this happen? Well, humans are naturally inquisitive, and perhaps an advert caught your eye while searching for 'The Ring' and you decided to look at it 'for a moment'. This advert led you to a whole set of discoveries that were intriguing. After several hours something in your subconscious made you think, 'Now the ring through the end of this pig's nose wasn't the sort of ring I started looking for'.

The same distractions can happen more subtly when you are working on the main feature of your project. You may be regularly losing time working on something that is not taking you forward towards your goal. For example, a common distraction in computer programming is 'making it look nice'. When you first see the results of your coding appear on the screen, it is natural for you to want to go back and improve the 'look and feel' of this interface. However, many programmers do this to the detriment of getting the program to *work* properly. As you might imagine, if the trend continues, this would not go down well with the examiners:

Examiner: So then, as far as I can see your program does not *do* what it is meant to do.
Student: True, but it really *looks* nice.

We are easily distracted, and we need help to maintain focus.

The importance of regular Manager meetings

To counteract our natural tendency to get distracted, it is important to find ways of involving your Manager. This can be done by learning to listen to that inner voice which says, 'remind me – *why* am I doing this?' A simple solution is to schedule a *daily* management meeting, where you review:

- the main aim and objectives
- the overall time-plan for the project
- how far you have progressed
- what is the most important thing you could be doing today?

Regular (but relatively short) meetings like this also help with your general motivation (see next section), as you take stock of the results of your work so far.

As an analogy, if you are walking in the countryside, climbing a hill in the rain, you will probably spend a lot of time looking at the ground watching carefully where you are placing your feet on the slippery ground. The irony of this is that even though you are steadily making progress, you do not notice because every step looks the same: 'footstep on muddy soil', 'footstep on muddy soil' . . . If however, you stop at regular intervals to look round, you will get a chance to take in the view. This not only shows you how far you have come, but is also rewarding in itself. Even a few steps forward can change your perspective. Some might say that looking around is the whole reason for taking the walk in the first place.

It is therefore important to mark regular slots in your diary when you will take stock of where you are. These are in addition to your daily management focus meetings. Figure 7.2 shows a series of questions that you could ask yourself about a month into your project. This is a self-assessment form whose main point is simply to get you to ask yourself a series of Manager-level focusing questions. However, you may wish to discuss your answers to the questions with your supervisor or focus group.

Project: Self-assessment form

Purpose: This form is intended to help you keep a top-level 'managerial' overview of your project, and to encourage you to think about the overall presentation and scheduling of the work.

1   State the major points of originality of the project.
2   What are the main *aims* of the project?
3   Give a *brief* summary of the work done so far.
4   How far do you feel this has taken you towards your main project goal?
5   Comment on your time management of the project workload.
6   Do you know yet what you would like to present in the final viva/demo?
7   What steps will you have to take to ensure that happens?
8   What 'risk management' plans do you have, to ensure you have *something consistent* to show if your final goals are not reached?
9   What areas of the project are you particularly worried about?
10   What steps are you taking to ensure these are addressed, and that you get support/help/information?
11   Are there any other comments which should be fed back to your supervisor?

Figure 7.2 Self-assessment form

Regular progress form

Name: _____   Date: _____

Progress since last meeting:

Summary of progress to date:

Actions for next week:

Other comments:

Figure 7.3 Example regular management reporting form

You might also want to develop and fill in your own management progress form (see Figure 7.3).

This can be used to give a regular (for example, fortnightly) report to your supervisor or focus group. Decide with your supervisor if this would be a useful method of reporting your work, and then plan in it your diary as a regular commitment. At the top (in the 'Progress since last meeting') you write down things you have achieved since your last meeting, and things you are still working on, specifically concentrating on the 'Actions' you *wrote down* on the previous form. This ensures that nothing is forgotten and that there is a consistent flow from one meeting to the next. The 'Summary of progress to date' is specifically designed to ensure that you consider your *whole* progress so far, since the start of the project. The 'Actions for next week' (or fortnight, or whatever) is a list of major targets that you are going to plan to achieve before the next meeting. Try to make these specific (e.g. 'Get all journal papers and produce a summary', rather than 'Make progress on literature review').

If used well, this sort of form can provide an invaluable way of regularly noting your progress and making executive decisions, knowing that someone else is expecting the report, and will read and comment on it.

Losing motivation

Everyone loses their motivation to work every now and again. This is not the same as 'getting stuck' or 'losing focus'. Getting *stuck* means that you *know* what you want but cannot see *how* to get it. Losing *focus* means that you are working away busily on the *wrong* things, that will not ultimately take you towards your goal. Losing *motivation* means that the very *act of working* becomes hard. If you find yourself making comments such as:

'I just *wish* this project was over!'

'*Why* do I have to get up this morning?'

'I just can't be *bothered* to do any work'

then you have probably lost your motivation, and you should take some time out straight away to sort out the problem.

These sort of comments are usually accompanied by feeling 'down' or tired. If this is a *change of state* for you (i.e. you were not like this a while ago, and this is not your normal personality), then you should take this as a warning signal from your mind and body that something needs to be addressed.

Finding your motivation

Maintaining motivation is often associated with *balance*. Work too *hard* and you will gradually become tired and dispirited. Work too *little* and you will know deep down that you are not making progress. This will affect your overall feeling of well-being and sense of self-worth.

The balance is to find the right combination of work and play that keeps life feeling fun, but also reassures you that you are on target and making measurable progress.

If you are tired, please take a break. You probably know this already, but pushing yourself to work when you are really tired can produce some bad work, and a feeling of resentment towards that work. If you take plenty of breaks and you are *still* feeling very tired, then you might wish to talk to someone about this – a friend, your supervisor, a counsellor or a doctor.

If, on the other hand, tiredness is not the problem (for example, you find that you have plenty of energy for *other* things) then you have probably lost your 'driving force' for working on your project. You need to take some time (at managerial level) to find that driving force.

If someone said, 'Get up at 5.00am tomorrow morning, write two pages, and then I'll give you a million pounds', you would probably find the motivation to get up and write. You might even be excited about it. If on the other hand the person told you instead to, 'Get up at 5.00am tomorrow morning, and write two pages because I told you so!', you would probably resent the whole experience. And yet the task (getting up and writing) is the same in both cases. This tells us that it is not usually the task *itself* that is the problem, but the picture you have in your head of *why* you are doing the task.

If you are not motivated to work, try looking at the task from different perspectives. Let us take the example that you are trying to write Chapter 3 of your final report, and you just cannot seem to get on with it. Assume that you are not stuck (i.e. you know *what* you should do) and are not particularly tired overall, you just feel as if you want to do anything but write this chapter.

Get your Manager to ask your Worker *why* the work is not getting done. Listen carefully to the answer – it might be something you can deal with straight away.

Manager:	Why don't you want to get on with this.
Worker:	I just don't feel like it.
Manager:	Why? What's the matter?
Worker:	It's too complex.
Manager:	Would a managerial meeting help? Maybe we could think about it a bit more and break it down into simpler tasks?

If this does not help, and the work plans are clear, we need to change the perspective to find the driving force. The first way of doing this is to raise the perspective by simply looking back at your overall plans. You might then see that according to your schedule, this chapter *needs* to be finished by the end of this week. This might be the push your Worker needs to get on with it.

If not, you may want to raise the perspective again – noting that the final report deadline is only three weeks away, and handing this in on time is important. You will know by the adrenaline rush whether you have found the motivating reason to start work on the chapter.*

If you are *still* having problems motivating yourself to start work, then you should raise the perspective yet again, and look at the negative consequences of not submitting the project report (failing the project, thus failing the degree, thus damaging a career path and so on). Imagine holding these possibilities in one hand in front of you. At the same time think of the positive consequences of doing the work (feeling of satisfaction, a good chapter, a report that is on time, a good qualification, the subsequent career and financial results). Hold these in the other hand. Weigh them up. Know that the difference between these two future possibilities really *does* come down to whether or not you do the next bit of work. This should help you to make a start.†

Someone else has done it already

A surprisingly common problem encountered by research students (who are trying to do something original) is the discovery (late into the project) of a paper or a product that appears to show that your work has already been done by someone else.

If this happens to you, you will immediately worry about the validity of your project. You may feel guilty or annoyed that you did not discover this before, for example, during the literature survey. You may even worry about the outcome of your project and the course. Stop. Relax. Make an appointment to talk to your supervisor.

Remember that if this happens, then you are not alone. For whatever reason, you embarked upon your project in good faith that it was original. Your supervisor knows this too and should be able to help you deal with this.

Sometimes you make the discovery yourself, and at other times someone else hands the paper to you, often with relish: 'Hey look

---

* This is the reason that some people have to wait until the last day before a deadline before starting on a piece of work. They need the panic of the upcoming deadline to motivate them to begin work. By far a better way is to induce *mild* panic on a regular basis by thinking through the project deliverables, so that you know that the chapter *has* to be written this week in order to achieve the final goal.

† If not, then you really should seek help urgently from your supervisor and other people to get some advice on what is holding you back.

what I found – it seems to be *exactly* what you are doing!' But, before you despair, let us just look at the positives in this situation.

- The fact that someone else is working on this topic helps to show that it is a worthy and worthwhile topic to study.
- You now have more literature (and a highly relevant piece of work at that), which you can include in your literature survey.
- No two people (or research groups) do the same thing. Imagine a person inventing the violin. Someone might have come up to them and said, 'Hey – I've got this great paper about an instrument with strings stretched over a wooden body. You should see this'. Imagine if the violin maker gave up because their friend had found this description of a guitar. Everyone's work is different.

Embrace the fact that other people are working on similar topics, and discuss with your supervisor how this might affect the focus of your work.

Running out of time

Everybody runs out of time in a project, and everyone seems to feel guilty about it. A good manager accepts that time ticks on and *will* run out. If your project is worthwhile there will always be more you can do with it, but time is finite, so you *are* going to run out of it. The key is to ensure that you run out of time *gracefully*.

You may wish to refer again to Chapter 5, which introduces storyboarding as an excellent project planning tool precisely because it is about order and flow, and *not* about absolute time-scales.

When you are in the final stages of the project, it is very important not to lose focus of the project as a whole. There can be a strong temptation to 'just carry on a bit longer to get this section of work finished'. Think about this for a moment – this is the Worker saying to the Manager, 'Don't bother me now. I know we might be short of time, but I know what's best; I have to complete this'. And there is the problem – you cannot get a high-level perspective when you are working on the ground.

Here is a warning that is taken from many years' experience of watching students in the final stages of their projects. Do not be driven to blindly finish what you are working on. Many a computing student has worked all hours to finish their computer program, apparently blind to the fact that it would be better to finalise their report. Of course the program is important, but the report is the statement to the examiners of what you have done and why you have done it. If the report is not complete you could fail – even with a working program! Now your Manager knows this, and has known it all along – it is written in your plan. But the Worker can sometimes take over near the end with disastrous consequences.

Here is a challenge for you to prevent the above from happening. Maybe when time is short you should have *more* management meetings, not fewer. This will help to ensure that, especially when the deadline is approaching, you focus on the essential things.

As an analogy, imagine you had to tidy a room and you had half an hour before someone important came in. You should keep taking time out to go to the door and pretend to be that person entering the room – and noting what is the most obvious thing to tidy up. When you run out of time, you know you will have done your best, and that the room is better than when you started. Beware the trap of getting really interested in sorting out a bookshelf in the far corner, and running out of time, not noticing that the important visitor will fall over a pile of smelly old clothes by the entrance.

The advice is clear. Do not abandon your Manager towards the end of a project when time is tight. Instead involve them *more* fully, having shorter meetings more often to ensure that the higher-level perspective guides the work being done, until the alarm clock strikes, and you can finally relax, knowing that you have done the best you could with the time available.

Summary

This chapter has taken you through a series of problems that are commonly encountered by people doing research projects, or indeed any form of complex work. The ideas given here will help you if you become stuck, or you lose focus, or indeed become unmotivated or dispirited with your work. If you discover some work that is very similar to yours, or you become aware that time is running out, then refer back to this chapter to help you to cope with the problem. But remember that this is just a starting-point, and that most people (when they encounter a problem) need to talk with someone about it. Be aware that talking about a problem is *not* somehow a sign of weakness, but is a sensible thing to do.

Your Manager and Worker will appreciate any advice from another perspective, such as your supervisor or focus group.

In the following chapter we look at the writing of the final report – perhaps the most important milestone and deliverable in any research project.

Chapter 8

The final report

Introduction

The final report for a research project may well be the biggest piece of creative writing you have ever done (and possibly ever will do). The companion book in this series (Berry, 2000) explains in more detail about the art and craft of composing a research paper. By contrast this chapter concerns making sure you *manage* the whole process effectively.

The final report is certainly highly important, and yet many people start work on it far too late, and fail to manage the process effectively because it is such a large task. This chapter guides you through the process of writing a large report. It encourages you to begin this process early, and advises on how to structure your sections and your writing time. There are some warnings from real-life experiences, accompanied by some principles which will maximise the effectiveness of your report, and ensure that your work has the best chance of being understood by those who are reading it or examining it.

Report-writing as an ongoing process

One of the biggest mistakes (and unfortunately one of the most common) is leaving the report write-up until the end of the project. This stems from the natural thought that you 'must finish your project, before you can write it'. However, the truth is that every project naturally falls into *phases*. These generally (but not always) include something similar to Figure 8.1.

Since each phase tends to conclude at a certain time (rather than continuing throughout the project) it is rather like having an

• Research • Specification of aims and objectives • Creative thoughts about how to tackle the project • Detailed design and planning • Practical execution of the project work • Testing, evaluation and refinement • Analysis and conclusion	Project time

Figure 8.1 Typical phases of a project

ordered series of mini-projects. These are likely to be closely related to any work packages you drew up in Chapter 5. It makes sense to make notes about each phase *while it is in progress*, then to write it up in its final form *as soon as the phase is complete*. There are several reasons that this is a good idea:

• Your brain can only actively hold so much information. You will forget crucial details if you do not write them down.

• The best time for writing notes on a subject is *while* you are thinking about it. If you leave it too long you will lose the details.

• At the very end of the project your mind is nearly always focused on 'fine-tuning' (e.g. serious computer code to get the program to work, auditions of your composition with feedback from others, analysing your test results, etc.). You may not easily remember, for example, the ten alternative design possibilities for your product that were so clear in your mind in the design phase.

• Writing an ongoing report is a good discipline that ensures you think deeply about each project phase, rather than just rushing on with the next one.

• Other people (such as your supervisor and focus group) can read what you have written and give you feedback, which may guide your project direction.

• Your supervisor, or another person, can also give you feedback on your writing style and report layout.

• You will get the satisfaction of seeing your report 'grow' as the project progresses. This also gives the reassurance that your most important deliverable is taking shape.

Therefore your report-writing should be scheduled into your management system as an ongoing process throughout the project. You should still allocate a special block of time for the report at the end of the project. This can be used for:

- Reviewing the report with the experience and perspective that can only be gained at the end of a project process.
- Proofreading (by yourself, and ideally by at least one other person).
- Writing the Conclusions and Abstract (typically the last things to be written).
- Printing (and binding if appropriate).

Some people find that scheduling a regular time (or times) each week throughout the project encourages them to get into the habit of writing up their work. Others build blocks of time into the larger-scale project plan, so that after completing a phase, there are several days put aside for writing it up. They often find this gives a useful sense of 'closure' on that phase, effectively shifting detailed information out of their brains onto paper, and leaving thinking space for the next phase. One thing is clear – it is never advisable simply to wait until you feel like writing. Experience seems to show that it never feels right and this can be fatal to a project.

Scoping your writing time

Whenever you choose to schedule your writing time, you will need to carefully *manage* the process. Some people rebel against such an idea, viewing writing as a creative task and, as such, not subject to management or organisation. However, creativity often needs a structure within which to operate.* You will use your time completely differently depending on what your mind is focused on. Imagine that you have scheduled a two-hour writing session and you sit down with one of the following mind-sets:

---

* Artists and writers often report that their greatest moments of creativity come about precisely because they carry out the discipline of scheduling regular times for writing (often at the same time each day) so that their brain and body can slot with ease into writing mode. The greatest musical performers can only play and perform and improvise with apparent effortlessness *because* they have practised for hours every day.

1   This is my hallowed writing time and is the time to be creative. I must produce excellent work, starting *now* . . .
2   In this two-hour slot I know that I need to make significant progress on Chapter 2. In particular I must review its structure, and then complete the writing of sections 1 and 2. Given that I have a total of two hours, I should spend 15 minutes on the structure, 45 minutes on section 1, take 15 minutes to relax, 45 minutes on section 2, and then 15 minutes to review what I've written.

Option 1 is what is really in many people's minds when they sit down to write. However they find it far too threatening when it comes to it. They sit looking at the page (or the computer screen) feeling distinctly guilty and uncreative. Writer's block usually happens when you are waiting for the inspiration to get you writing. Many writers say that they have to *just start writing* to overcome such a block.

Maybe option 2 appears a bit too organised for some, but it demonstrates the awareness of a grander plan. It implies that the author (Manager) has creatively organised the report, is aware of the contents and the sub-sections, has worked out the total amount of writing time available, and has allocated certain sections to be written at certain times.

There are two benefits that spring directly from such an approach.

1   During each of the 45-minute writing slots there is no need to worry about *anything else* other than writing the current section. The Worker is reassured that the management has everything in control, and so he or she can concentrate on the job at hand.
2   You know you have 45 minutes to write a particular section, and you can aim to get it finished within that time.

This concept of 'writing to a fixed time' is very useful. Some people insist they take as long as is necessary to write a particular section. These are usually the same people who run late and miss their deadlines. If you know you have a fixed time, you can take a range of approaches to ensure that the section gets finished on time.

•   If the section is quite open-ended and you just need to 'discuss the topic', you can simply start writing, and (rather like an exam) just stop writing when the time is up.

- If there are a number of definite points that need to be addressed within a section, then you should take a more structured approach. Start off by typing in the main points in brief, maybe even as bullet-points. Then, go back and write a 'killer sentence' for each point; one that perfectly sums up the concept. If there is time, then go back again from the top and expand on each killer sentence – making it the start of a paragraph. Keep going, refining your work and adding more material until the time runs out.

Whichever method you use, just stop writing when the time is up. Briefly look over your work, noting down anything you wish to change later. Then schedule time for *later* (ideally on another day), to read it through and make corrections.

Contents as a springboard for writing

Most students nowadays are used to working with a word processor. If you are not yet familiar with the use of a computer for writing, then this is the time to learn. Even though there are several very good reasons for working with pen on paper,* the advantages of word-processing are numerous:

- Your final report needs to be printed, so save time and work in that medium by typing things up from the beginning.
- Copies can be made easily (actually safer than a single piece of hand-written work).
- Work can be emailed to people for information and review.
- It is much easier to experiment with your structure by moving around blocks of text, as opposed to re-writing various sections or physically cutting and pasting pieces of paper.
- Certain useful functions are built-in, such as spelling checks and word counts.

A particularly good way of structuring a report is to type in the contents page at the earliest opportunity. Discuss this with your

---

* The physicality of pen or pencil and paper can cause you to think in different ways to using a computer. This is particularly good at the ideas stage, where you can utilise the free-space on a page of paper to jot down ideas, concepts, diagrams, and topic links (see the section on mind-mapping in Chapter 3).

supervisor and focus group, and refine the structure. Then make a copy of the file. This copy then becomes your working report. The Contents file might have contained this:

Chapter 8: The Final Report

Introduction

Report-writing as an ongoing process

Scoping your writing time

This becomes the template for chapter 8, where the writing for each section is allocated a particular time-slot. In this way the report is gradually built up, following the model of the contents page. As you write, inevitably your ideas will develop and the structure may change, in which case you should adjust the original Contents file accordingly.

Some writers use a method where every section has its writing slot marked in the file, like this:

Chapter 8: The Final Report (Week 4)

Introduction (Monday: 9.00–9.30)

Report-writing as an ongoing process (Monday: 9.30–10.30)

Scoping your writing time (Tuesday: 9.30–10.30)

Just like the storyboard concept, and your overall project plans, you are not to be *ruled* by these time-slots. It is just that experience shows that for most people a disciplined, carefully planned schedule is more likely to yield success than total freedom.

Establishing the readership

The main message of Chapter 6 was to think carefully about the person (or people) you are trying to communicate with, and then to reveal your information from what they *already* know to what you *want* them to know. The same is true for a final report. So it is vital that you develop an understanding of *for whom* the report is written. Too often students assume it is written *for* their supervisor who might well be an expert in the subject area. Accordingly, such writing often misses out explanations that would make the report more understandable and useful to a wider audience.

Instead of writing personally for your supervisor, ask him or her to explain to you who your target audience is. I often recommend imagining a fellow student who has done most of your course, but knows *nothing* about your specific project. Therefore you need not waste valuable space and time covering details that are clearly outlined in textbooks or course notes, but instead can concentrate on revealing the information that you have discovered during your particular project. This has two added benefits:

1 Your supervisor (or any other examiner) will be able to judge what you have learnt *beyond* the taught course.
2 Your report will be readily usable for future students because you have written it for that particular knowledge set.

It is good to have a *specific* person in mind as you are writing, so you can ask questions such as, 'Would Jim know what I'm talking about here?' Imagine you are at the beginning of one of the 45-minute writing sessions mentioned above, and you know that you need to cover a section called 'The future of transistors'. If you are stuck as to what to write, just try visualising 'Jim' sitting in front of you. Your job is to explain to him the future of transistors, and you have not got long to do it. Try imagining the conversation in your head, and type up what you say to Jim. This will naturally be at the right level because he is your typical 'target audience' and you know roughly what he already understands. You can probably start with an overview of the topics that will need to be covered (and these will become your bullet-points). You can then explain each point in turn, and write down the killer sentences; these are the single concepts that Jim needs to hear in order to understand what you are saying. Then you can go back and explain in more detail.

Do not worry too much about the writing style being too conversational; this can be corrected later. Often when you re-read something (especially the following day) you realise that certain phrases should be expressed differently. However, it is better to succeed at explaining your concept in a relaxed style, rather than having beautifully structured prose that your readers cannot understand.

House styles

Check with your academic institution or department whether there are particular writing or formatting rules that you need to follow. They may allow you to choose the style, but you should check to see if there are restrictions on line-spacing, text-size, use of headings, use of numbering, formatting of figures, and referencing styles (see Chapter 4). There may be rules to follow about writing style, e.g. whether to write in first person ('I carried out the following experiment'), or third person ('the following experiment was carried out').

The earlier you discover these guidelines, the better. If you are using a word-processor you can then produce a writing *template*, which contains the appropriate paper layout and font styles, etc.

If there are no specific guidelines, it is still wise to discuss the format with your supervisor. Look at various books and journal papers, and previous reports from your institution, to find out what is permissible and to see what you prefer.

Revealing information to the reader

Those of you familiar with, and maybe good at, novel writing or poetry know that language can be used to maintain suspense. The reader can be kept waiting, basking in a flow of words that sets the scene and builds the tension. When writing for information, however, it is better to use plainer language that carries your reader logically through your argument, and unveils the information you wish to portray in a sensible order. In Chapter 6 we discussed the art of giving a talk, and how to reveal information to your audience in a logical way. In the section 'Planning the presentation' we saw how much can be learnt from the way a TV documentary captures the audience's interest, maintains their imagination, and leads them through a series of logical steps supported by sound and vision.

You may wish to revisit Chapter 6 in the context of writing your final report, in order to think again about how other people's minds work. What is in your head at the moment you start writing should be as close as possible to what you think will be in your readers' heads when they start reading.

Appendices

You can place material in an appendix if you want your reader to be *aware* of it, but not *forced* to read it as part of the main body of the report. In other words, if you have things which you and your supervisor agree should be included in the report, but that seems to interrupt the 'flow' of the report, then consider putting them in an appendix. Label your appendices alphabetically.

Many authors use *Appendix A* to be their list of references. Likewise *Appendix B* is often the bibliography (i.e. a list of books and papers that have influenced your work and writing, but are not necessarily referenced nor quoted from).

Other uses of appendices include:

- Questionnaire forms (the summary goes in the main body, but the detailed responses from your survey can be kept in an appendix).
- Relevant correspondence (e.g. from an expert in your topic area).
- Information (such as printouts of web pages or adverts) which has influenced your work, but would look wrong inserted in the main body of the report.
- Computer code listings (although these are increasingly being submitted electronically, see next section).

Ensure that details of your appendices are listed in your contents page.

Submitting electronic information

Nowadays many final reports are submitted with a disk (such as a CD-ROM or a DVD), which provides information in electronic form. Here are the sorts of information that typically go on such a disk:

- an electronic copy of the report (i.e. the computer files from your word processor that made up the report);
- computer code (source files, libraries and executables);
- web pages (text and images) from your literature survey;
- sound files of musical compositions or other sound examples;
- video demonstrations of the product in action.

The electronic copy of your report is especially useful as it can be sent via email, edited into a publication (see Chapter 10), and stored in a much smaller space than the paper version. Computer code takes up a lot of printed space, and is inherently more useful to future students if available ready-to-use on a disk. If you have found useful information on web pages (particularly that which is not stored in published, printed form) it is good to store those pages in electronic form on your disk. This is because the web is a precarious place for storing information – web addresses can change and sites can disappear completely, and it would be a shame to lose relevant information. Any media, which are not text or static graphics, can be included. Video demonstrations of your product in action show the examiners that it works, and allow you to control the filming conditions. You can also include sound or music examples to illustrate points throughout your report.

A good electronic appendix should be fully indexed, both on its cover and within the printed report. If, for example, you are referring to sound examples from within your text you might be advised to include the reference as follows:

> Beethoven used the oboe as a solo bridge in the 5th symphony [CD track 4]

Or if you are referring to a file on the CD (e.g. a web page) use something like this:

> This information is available on the accompanying CD [/research/sound/index.htm]

This implies that you have structured the CD in a sensible way, using carefully named folders and sub-folders to hold the information in a logical place.

As with standard printed appendices, ensure that details of the contents of your disk are listed in your contents page. If it contains too many individual items, then produce a high-level index that outlines the most important folders on the disk.

As a final point, you should always ensure that the report can be read *without* the accompanying disk, should it get lost or damaged. The disk should enhance the report and offer further insights into the project.

Summary

Chapter 4 considered the literature survey in some detail, and included a section on how to handle references, and warnings about plagiarism. These apply also to the final report, which this chapter has considered in more detail. We have seen the importance of managing the final report as a series of ongoing mini-projects throughout the project's lifetime. We have looked at how to plan your writing time, and how to address the appropriate readership. We have briefly considered the house styles that may be required for your particular report, and outlined the main uses of electronic submissions to accompany your report.

After your report is completed and handed in, there is often a verbal exam (a 'viva'), and this is the subject of the next chapter.

Chapter 9

The viva voce examination

Introduction

Many research projects culminate not only with the handing in of a written report, but in a time of active discussion with the examiners. This chapter guides you through the preparation for such an encounter, and helps you to understand what the examiners are looking for. Such examinations are traditionally called viva voce* (or 'viva' for short), and take place by word of mouth, rather than in written form. However, a viva is by no means a simple spoken replacement for a conventional written exam, but rather a meeting of minds, and an opportunity for you to discuss the significance of your work in detail.

Purpose of the viva

Let us consider the reasons for holding a viva, both from the examiners' point of view, and your own.

From the point of view of the examiners, the purpose of a viva is to:

- Establish that the written report they have read *belongs* to the person sitting in front of them!
- Clarify anything in the report which is unclear.
- Determine the extent to which the student understands the contents of the report.

---

* From the Medieval Latin meaning 'with the living voice' (*The Oxford Compact Dictionary*, 1996, OUP).

- Challenge the student's ideas, to determine how strongly or deeply the student believes them.
- Engage in general discussions around the topic area, to determine how flexible the student's thought processes are.

From *your* point of view the purpose of the viva is to:

- Ensure that the examiners comprehend the main purpose of your project and its most significant results.
- Show that you understand not only what you have written, but also issues surrounding the general topic area.
- Engage in conversation with someone who has read your work in detail.
- Clarify any misunderstandings about what you have written.

A few observations flow directly from the above points:

- The work you submit must be all yours, or properly annotated as someone else's.
- Anything you write is open to questioning and further discussion.
- You should *expect* to be challenged, and you have the right to answer.

The degree of *challenge* will be different according to your level in the education system. Viva exams at doctoral level are often called 'thesis defences', where it is understood that someone (or indeed a group of people) will somehow attack or challenge the central tenet of your work in order to determine just how rigorous your thoughts and research procedures have been. You should spend considerable time in preparing for such a process, with your supervisor, your focus group, and with other people who have already been through such a process themselves. It really is not as bad as it might first sound. Most people emerge from their doctoral vivas quite tired, but *glad* they went through the process, and pleased to have engaged with people who really understood what they were talking about.

At masters level, there is usually less emphasis on 'defending your corner', and more on demonstrating that you understand the *significance* of what you have done, and how this fits in to the other work that has been done in this area.

At undergraduate level, you will still be challenged, but the main focus is on asking you to describe the *details* of your work, and on clarifying any misunderstandings.

However, at whatever level you are working, you should be prepared for challenging questions, and also those that appear to go off the subject. Also be ready for 'shifts of gear' in the questioning. For example, you might be asked the following five questions, one after the other:

- On page 14, you say '. . .', but this appears to contradict what Roxburgh says about it in his well-respected journal paper. How do you respond to that?
- Please explain how this (*pointing to the page*) bit of code works.
- What for you is the most significant finding of your research?
- Which paper in your literature survey is the most relevant to your work, and why?
- How do you see the future of this field of study progressing in the next 10 years?

Note how the 'level' of the questions changes; from a direct challenge, to low-level specifics, to a high-level overview, to engagement with the literature, through to speculation about the future. Now a real viva would probably operate with more of a conversational flow, but nevertheless the style of the questions may change as rapidly as above.

Preparation for the viva

As you will gather from the depth of the questioning to be expected at a viva, you must take time to prepare for it. Some people go in without preparation thinking, 'If I don't know it now I never will'. Still others try to somehow 'learn' their report, as if they were revising for a written exam. Neither of these is an appropriate way of preparing for the viva.

What you actually need to do is to practise *talking* about your work with people who are reasonably knowledgeable about the subject area, and to become confident at answering *questions* on your work. One of the best ways of doing this is to plan several sessions with your focus group (ideally with your supervisor in attendance).

Take turns in your supervision group to play the role of 'the examiners' and 'the person in the viva'. It is quite important for you to get some practice at formulating questions and comments as if you were an examiner. After all an examiner is not some specially gifted individual, but rather a person who is attempting to interact with you and assess your work. So try asking each other questions about your work. At first your mind might be a blank, but try the following sorts of questions to begin with, then later invent your own:

- What have you achieved overall on your project?
- Which part of the work are you most proud of?
- How can you reassure me that your tests are reliable?
- Explain that section in more detail.
- Which parts of your work could be published, and where?

When I have run mock vivas with a focus group, it has always been amusing to see the range of responses from students who are pretending to be examiners. Some people do not seem to be able to ask a question. 'Er – I just can't think of anything to ask'. Others seem to relish the new sense of power. 'Ha Ha,' rubbing hands together, and smiling with an evil grin, 'your statistical analysis bears no relationship to the well-known guidelines. Why not?' However, most people find that they benefit from being made to think of questions, and indeed to answering questions delivered in a manner that an examiner would never dream of.

When you have answered all these questions, and more, and you are feeling comfortable with the process, then you are probably ready for your viva.

Figure 9.1 shows a self-assessment form (similar to the one used in Chapter 7, Figure 7.2) which will help you to focus on the latter stages of your project, including the viva.

Presentation time within the viva

In Figure 9.1, the second question implies that you have some say over the structure of the viva. Sometimes the viva's structure is published and known. At other times it is entirely up to the examiners. Whichever is true, you will probably be given an opportunity to explain your work, and it is important that you plan for this.

Project: Self-assessment form 2

Purpose: This form is intended to think about the submission of the report, and the viva.

1   What is your understanding of the purpose of the viva?
2   Explain how you plan to run the viva.
3   What equipment will you require, if any?
4   What sorts of questions do you think you'll be asked?
5   Which questions do you fear the most?
6   How do you plan to deal with them?
7   How much of the report have you completed?
8   What plans do you have to ensure that the report is completed on time?
9   Are you submitting any media (e.g. CD-ROM), and if so, what will it include?
10 How do you plan to use the time between the report submission and the viva?

Figure 9.1 Self-assessment form to guide you through the project's final weeks

Some viva exams formally include a presentation time (say 20 minutes) before the questioning. At others, the examiners may begin by saying, 'Give us a 5 or 10 minute overview of what your work is all about and what it has achieved'. This is your chance to set the agenda for the discussion, so it is important that you prepare for it.

If it is a formal presentation, then you may wish to prepare a proper slideshow as described at the end of Chapter 6. If it is an explanation around the table, then it is better that you prepare some cards containing the main points that you wish to communicate. Even in the event that the examiners do *not* give you this opportunity, you will not regret the preparation. Imagine if you have two postcards containing every main point you want to get across, then the examiners say, 'Well, we're nearly finished; is there anything you feel we have not covered?' Rather than the (usual) response, 'Er, no, I don't think so', you could scan down your main points and say something like 'I think we've covered most things, but I don't think I've stressed this well enough . . .'

So, the sorts of things your notes (or talk) should cover are:

• the main focus of your study
• why this is important
• what you have done/studied/proven/challenged

- how your work relates to that of others
- the significance of what you have achieved
- the weaknesses or limitations of your work*
- the novelty of your work
- the potential future implications of your work.

Summary

The viva examination should be seen as an *opportunity* for you to talk in detail about the project you have been working on for a long period of time. After all by now you are something of an expert! To maximise your chances of getting your message across to the examiners, you will need to practise talking about your project with others. The more you can cultivate an atmosphere where you ask and respond to probing and challenging questions about your work, the more confident you will be when it comes to the viva itself.

---

* It is *not* seen as a negative or damaging thing to talk about potential weaknesses in your work. It shows careful and objective analysis and is seen as being honest. This is much better than claiming that your work is better than it really is.

Chapter 10

Publishing your results

Introduction

The final chapter considers the options available to you for publishing your work. It looks at the different types of publication, and gives some general advice about how to get your work published.

Why publish?

The writing and publication of academic papers is a central part of higher education practice. As a student you may be aware only of the *teaching* commitments of the staff (the lectures, seminars, exams and marking). However, it is *research* that is often the driving force behind much of the work done by universities and colleges.

One of the natural outcomes of finding out something new is telling others about it; hence the need for publication. What is perhaps less obvious (from the point of view of students) is how important the activity of publication becomes, because it is used as a *measure* of creativity, productivity, and esteem in the academic community. Various exercises are in existence that link publication performance (amongst other things) to personal pay, promotion opportunities, departmental grants and overall university funding. The resulting figures contribute to 'league tables', which rank higher education institutions, and influence funding bodies and potential parents and students, thus determining future funding and admissions.

Like it or not, publication is vital to the academic community. If you wish to continue to be involved in academic life after your current studies, then consideration of publication will play an important part in what you do.

For now, you need to consider whether or not you should publish the work you have just completed.

Should you publish?

Once you have completed your report, and have successfully come through the viva examination, you may wonder who else will read your report. First, if your report has been bound it is likely to be available in your department for future students to borrow and look at. Higher level reports (most doctoral and some masters) are often kept in the university library, which means that they are available to all at the university and can also be requested by other universities via inter-library loans.

If, however, you (and your supervisor) are convinced that your work deserves to be seen by a wider audience, then you will need to consider publication. The first thing you should be aware of is that getting work into print is not an easy process. It is a time-consuming and mentally challenging procedure, which usually involves the following stages:

- selecting a publication to target (e.g. a specific journal)
- finding out about the specific writing requirements of that publication
- deciding which sections of your work are going to be put forward for that publication
- editing a draft paper and creating an abstract
- sending the abstract to the editor, and awaiting a reply
- sending in the draft, and waiting for the referees' comments
- re-working the paper according to the referees' recommendations
- working with the commissioning editors to finalise the wording and layout.

The whole process can take a long time, even assuming your paper is accepted at each of the above stages. The writing and editing tasks are also quite significant – as you cannot just cut out chunks of your report and bolt them into a new document. Therefore you need to make sure:

- that you have got the *time* available to commit to this (many students hand in their report, have their viva, then leave and go on to something else);
- that your work contains enough *novelty* for publication (discussions with your supervisors and with other experts in the area will help you to determine this);
- that you really *want* to do this.

This last point is very important. You should have a strong reason for wanting to get your work published. For example, you may want to work for an organisation where your publication record is important. On the other hand, it may be that you have discovered something you believe in so strongly that you simply *must* get it 'out there'. The whole task of publication takes time and effort, so you should be sure that the benefits gained from getting your work into print would be worth that effort.

Which publication?

Every journal or publisher is different – with its own focus, readership, style of writing and presentation. Some students are so proud of their masters or doctoral thesis that they naturally think they have 'already written a book'. Editors are very wary of taking student work directly, and methods such as converting your thesis into a book, or taking a chapter out of it to make a paper, will rarely work. The report you have written so far (as described in Chapter 8) has been written for a particular reader, for a particular purpose, within specific style and page-limit. Everything is different for an external publication. The companion book to this (Berry, 2000) covers this problem in more detail, and stresses the fact that you will have to radically re-write everything you have already written. Having recently spent so much time writing a huge document, the last thing you may feel like doing is *more writing*, especially re-working what you have just completed.

If you decide that publication really *is* for you, you will then need to consider the *type* of publication.

Chapter 4 described the various types of publication, and how each addresses the reviewing process, highlighting the trade-off between refereeing quality and publication turnaround time. For an academic publication you are probably choosing between a conference paper, a journal paper, or a book.

Conference publication

You may decide that a conference is the best way to present your work to the world. Most conferences advertise their key topics and important dates on their own web site (found easily by typing the conference name into an Internet search engine). The first deadline is usually for a paper to be submitted. Therefore you need to organise your writing so that this deadline can be met. You often have to write the full paper *before* you have any idea of whether your paper will be accepted for the conference or not.

Remember to write for a *specific* conference by reading carefully what the web site says about the sort of delegates it attracts, and by talking to those people you know who know about it, or ideally who have presented a paper there in previous years. You can learn a lot about the 'feel' of a conference from finding out about the atmosphere there, or the social events, or the type of people who attend. Remember that by going to a conference you will gain opportunities to meet other people working in your subject area. These personal links can become very important for your future work. You will also gain experience in how to present a paper in front of an international audience, and of course hearing about what other people are doing in your topic around the world.

At a future date you will be given an acceptance or rejection for your paper. Even if it is an acceptance, there may be a list of corrections or suggestions for improvement from referees. A second date will be listed on the web site which is when the 'camera-ready' paper needs to be submitted. This is a finalised and properly formatted version with all illustrations in place.

You will need to register for the conference (fees vary widely), find out about travel arrangements, and liaise with the conference organisers about presentation facilities (such as the availability of computers and loudspeakers). A first conference can feel like a daunting experience, but most junior researchers have found it to be very rewarding, and they have returned feeling somewhat 'grown up', proud that they have presented their work in public and had detailed discussion with the international representatives of their topic area.

Journal and book publication

For most journal papers you send a full paper, so first of all you have to write the material you wish to get published! Some, however, require you to first send only an abstract, on which they will make an initial decision about whether to ask you for a full paper.

With your supervisor, you should explore a list of relevant journals, and then get hold of a few copies of each journal. Read the papers, the editorial, and most importantly the instructions for authors. These will often cover the journal's aims and objectives, describe the target audience, and give details about how to write for the journal and how to format your paper.

For a book, try contacting various publishing houses and discuss with them the need for a new book in your area. Prepare for many rounds of discussion and refusals, as publishers are looking for things that they *know* will sell. If the topic area is of interest to a publisher they may ask you to fill in a detailed Book Proposal. In this you will probably be asked to give some or all of the following information:

- a detailed overview of the intended readership
- some 'blurb' which could appear on the cover
- an outline of your book's contents
- a sample chapter
- an idea of the length of the book, number of figures, and any special publication requirements (e.g. special size, or CD attached)
- a date when the final manuscript could be complete
- an analysis of the book's competitors
- names of referees who would be able to review your proposal.

Nowadays there are many opportunities for self-publishing, but the pros and cons of this are hard to generalise and you should discuss this with your supervisor.

If you have decided to publish your work in a journal or a book, there is nothing quite like the thrill of seeing your work finally in print, in the official binding. However, as we discussed earlier, it takes a lot of effort to get to this point, so you really want to be sure that the process will benefit you.

Summary

This chapter assumes that you have made it to the end of a successful project, and are now considering publishing your work. We have looked at some of the questions you should ask yourself before committing to a publication and have stressed the importance of writing the material especially for the chosen publication, not just taking it from your report.

In this book, we have seen that the management of a research project is a complex process that demands *much* self-management. If you have invested the time to put some of these ideas into practice you will find, like me, that they flow over into everyday life, and can improve how you operate in other areas of your life. If you wish to tune your skills still further, please look at the references in the Bibliography for some ideas for further reading.

I would like to conclude by wishing you every success with whatever you choose to do next.

Bibliography

Allen, D., *Getting Things Done: The Art of Stress-free Productivity*, London: Piatkus Books, 2002.

Berry, R., *The Research Project – How to Write it*, London: Routledge, 2000.

Buzan, T. and Buzan, B., *The Mind Map Book: How to Use Radiant Thinking to Maximize your Brain's Untapped Potential*, London: BBC Books, 1993 (see also www.mind-map.com).

Godefroy, C. H. and Clark, J., *The Complete Time Management System*, London: Piatkus Books, 1991.

McGee-Cooper, A., *Time Management for Unmanageable People*, New York/London: Bantam Doubleday Dell, 1994.

Mindjet: *MindManager* software from: http://www.mindjet.com/uk/, last viewed August 2004.

Morgenstern, J., *Time Management from the Inside Out*, London: Hodder & Stoughton General, 2001.

Thompson, P., 'Conversation: the power of persuasion', Audio tape series: Nightingale Conant, 2000.